D1028171

Exploring the Old Testament in the New

Exploring the Old Testament in the New

PETER R. RODGERS

RESOURCE *Publications* · Eugene, Oregon

EXPLORING THE OLD TESTAMENT IN THE NEW

Resource Publications
An Imprint of Wipf and Stock Publishers
199 W. 8th Ave., Suite 3
Eugene, OR 97401

www.wipfandstock.com

ISBN 13: 978-1-602032-257-4

Manufactured in the U.S.A.

To Steve, Jon, and Sarah

Contents

Preface

THE CAREFUL READER OF the New Testament will notice how frequently the Old Testament is quoted or alluded to by these earliest Christian writers. Whether it is a quotation introduced by a formula like "as it is written," or an allusion or echo of the Hebrew Scriptures embedded in the writing, on almost every page of the New Testament we find some reference to the Old Testament. It is safe to say that it is difficult to understand the New Testament documents without an understanding of the varied ways in which they make use of the Old Testament. The quotations are especially easy to spot, since they are indented and printed in poetic lines in our modern bibles, such as the NIV or the NRSV, or are printed in italics in the Common English Bible. Take, for example, the quotation from Psalm 78:2 at Matthew 13:35, where the Psalm is cited as scriptural support for Jesus' teaching in parables:

> 35. This was to fulfill what has been spoken through the
>   prophet:
>   "I will open my mouth to speak
>   in parables;
>   I will proclaim what has been
>   hidden from the
>   foundation of the world." (NRSV)

To begin this study you may find it valuable to spend a few minutes thumbing through the NRSV or the NIV and noting all those places where the larger quotations from the Old Testament are set out in indented and poetic form like the one illustrated above. Most printed modern editions will also give a footnote, indicating where the quotation can be found in the Old Testament.

This book is written to be a practical guide for serious students of the Bible, who want to explore the richness of the use of the Old Testament in the New. The contemporary study of this phenomenon, at least in the English-speaking world, can be dated to C. H. Dodd's book, *According to the Scriptures*. This book appeared in 1952, and was followed by a number of other studies on the use of the Old Testament in individual books. Some of these studies will be referred to in the pages that follow. The disciplined exploration of the use of the Old Testament in the New Testament has attracted considerable interest, and has warranted the recent publication of a large volume devoted to the subject. The *Commentary on the New Testament Use of the Old Testament*, edited by G. K. Beale and D. A. Carson provides a valuable and up-to-date resource for those wishing to pursue this study.

Several terms used in this book are commonly employed by scholars who work in the use of the Old Testament in the New, and it will be important for the reader to have clearly in mind how they are used. These terms are:

Quotations: This term refers to Old Testament passages which are used by a New Testament writer, and introduced by an introductory formula such as "as it is written," (Rom 1:17) or Matthew's recurrent use of the formula introducing quotations: "All this took place to fulfill what had been spoken by the Lord through the prophet . . ." (Matt 1:23, 2:6, 2:15, etc.). Some Old Testament passages are clearly quotations, but have only the shortest introduction. For example, in 1 Pet 1:24, what is clearly a conscious quotation from Isa 40:6–8, is introduced with only one word "for" (διότι). And in the same letter at 3:10, a quotation from Ps 34:12–16 is introduced with only the word "for" (γάρ). But there can be no doubt that the writer is consciously quoting the Old Testament passage.

Allusions: An allusion is an indirect reference to an Old Testament passage that has been incorporated into the New Testament writing. A good example is 1 Pet 2:21–25, where Peter cites a number of phrases from Isa 53, but makes no reference to the text as coming from Isaiah's fourth servant song: "He committed no sin, no deceit was found in his mouth . . . etc." There is no doubt that Peter is referring consciously to Isaiah 53, and that his readers or auditors would be expected to recognize the reference. The Book of Revelation has no quotations from the Old Testament introduced with a formula. But it is widely recognized that there are many scripture allusions and echoes throughout the book.

Echoes: This term has been used by many scholars to refer to Old Testament references that are embedded in the New Testament, but are less extensive, or less obvious than allusions. Indeed, some scholars use the two terms interchangeably. But the term "echoes" has received much more attention since the publication of Richard Hays' *Echoes of Scripture in the Letters of Paul* in 1989. An echo is a scripture reference that may be recognized by as little as a phrase or a word. But that phrase or word serves to evoke for the writer and reader alike a whole passage of the Old Testament. Thus, as Hays has shown, the expression in Rom 3:20, "for no human being will be justified in his sight," is an echo of Ps 143:2. However, it is not just the language of the verse, but also the logic of the whole psalm that is evoked by the citation. Similarly, by adding the word "exodus" (ἔξοδον) to the story of the transfiguration, Luke refers to a story at the heart of Israel's history. This addition evokes for writer and readers the story of the exodus of Israel from Egypt. One word echoes a larger story.

Narratives: At certain points it is clear that whole stories or passages of the Old Testament have influenced and shaped the New Testament writings. Psalm 23, which begins, "The Lord is my Shepherd," has almost certainly influenced Jesus' parable of the Prodigal Son in Luke 15 and his teaching on the "good shepherd" in John 10.[1] The Narrative of Hannah in 1 Samuel 1–2 has shaped the way the story of Nativity of Jesus has been told in Luke 1.[2] Many proposals have been made regarding the way Old Testament narratives have shaped the New Testament writings, and some of them will be reviewed in this book.

1. Bailey, *Lost*, 194–212.
2. Wright, *New Testament*, 379.

Intertextuality: This term refers to a relationship that a writer may intend or a reader may find between two texts. In this study, it refers to a web of relationships that exist between a text (or texts) in the Old Testament and a New Testament writer. For the writer, the reference may be conscious or subconscious. For the reader, it may be clear, faint or almost unrecognizable. But for any relationship that may be discerned between the older text and the later text, the term *intertextuality* is a valuable designation. For example, in 1 Cor 2:16 Paul writes, "For who has known the mind of the Lord so as to instruct him? But we have the mind of Christ." Paul is clearly citing Isa 40:13, although he does not recognize it as a quotation from scripture. Whether or not his readers/hearers were able to catch the reference, an intertextual relationship exists here between Isaiah and Paul.

HOW TO USE THIS BOOK

This book is intended to be a practical guide, and is written in a conversational style. The student will need to have a modern translation of the Bible. The New Revised Standard Version (NRSV) is the English translation most commonly used. The New International Version (NIV) will also be referred to, as well as the Common English Bible (CEB). The references to the Greek will be from the Nestle-Aland twenty-seventh Edition (NA27) or the United Bible Societies Fourth Edition (UBS4). Resources for studying the Hebrew Bible (BHS) and the Septuagint (LXX) can be found online at the website of the German Bible Society.[3] The New English Translation of the Septuagint (NETS) will be a very helpful resource. For the Dead Sea Scrolls, the translation that is used is Geza Vermes, *The Complete Dead Sea Scrolls in English.* Although knowledge of Greek and Hebrew will be important for thorough exploration of the use of the Old Testament in the New Testament, this book is presented in such a way that students without knowledge of the original languages of the Bible can derive considerable benefit from

---

3. http://www.dbg.de/en/meta/home.html.

the study. It may also provide incentive for learning the biblical languages.

Each of the eight chapters that follow treats a different aspect of the use of the Old Testament in the New. These areas of investigation and some of the questions they raise are as follows:

Form: What is the text-form of the quotation in the New Testament? Is it similar or different to the form of the text found in the Old Testament? Are there any variations in the textual tradition (i.e. the numerous manuscripts) of either the Old Testament or the New Testament? Are the differences in the texts accidental or intentional?

Introduction: Many Old Testament quotations in the New Testament are introduced with a formula such as "As it is written," or "This took place to fulfill what was spoken through the prophet. . ." Other quotations lack an introductory formula. Many words or phrases from the Old Testament are embedded in a New Testament passage, and the reader would need to know the scripture well in order to hear the echo. Therefore we need to be alert to the implications of the presence or absence of an introductory formula in the New Testament writing.

Selection: A very important question for the student of the Old Testament in the New is why was this or that particular Old Testament text selected. Where two or more Old Testament passages are combined together, what was the principle or theme that caused the New Testament writer to bring them together? The reason for selection is not always obvious, and careful attention to the exegetical practices that caused the writer to select certain texts can prove surprisingly fruitful.

Application: Some Old Testament texts used by the New Testament writers are applied to several different features of the Christian story. For example, verses from Isaiah's Fourth Servant Song (Isaiah 53) are applied to Jesus' healing ministry (Matt 8:17) or to Christ's death as an offering for sin (Mark 10:45). Both applications of the chapter are brought together in 1 Peter 2, where the primary purpose for citing from this passage is to encourage Christians to follow the example of Christ's non-retaliation under trial. What can we learn from the different ways in which the New Testament writers apply an Old Testament passage?

Combination: We often find Old Testament texts from different contexts brought together by the New Testament writers. For example, in Romans 10:19–21 Paul brings together texts from several places in the Old Testament (Psalm 18, Deuteronomy 32, Isaiah 65). Can we discover the background and purpose that would have led Paul to have drawn these texts together into his argument in this way?

History: Many of the Old Testament texts used by New Testament writers were also cited in other Jewish writings of the period. For some of these texts there is a rich history of interpretation in Israel before the rise of Christianity. The study of comparative exegesis, and the history of interpretation within Judaism can help to set the context and deepen our understanding of the New Testament writers' use of these scripture texts.

Story: The study of the Old Testament in the New often reveals the larger narrative of God and his people that underlies both testaments. Thus the study of the Old Testament quotations allusions and echoes can provide a lens through which to view that narrative. This study can train us to read scripture as a coherent story.[4]

Function: When we find a quotation, allusion or echo of the Old Testament in the New, we need to ask how it functions for the New Testament writing. Are Old Testament texts merely brought in as proof texts, to confirm a point made by the writer, or do these citations make a more substantial contribution to the thought of the writer? Does the Old Testament passage exercise a constitutive, shaping function for the writing? Do the Old Testament texts shape the thought of the writer? Is the New Testament author using the Old Testament as a "grab bag of isolated oracles," to quote Richard Hays,[5] or does the appearance of a text in a gospel or epistle indicate a long and careful process of meditation and study of the scriptures of Israel on the part of the New Testament writer?

---

4. Bauckham, "Reading Scripture as a Coherent Story." 38–53.

5. Hays, *Conversion*, 48.

I am grateful to the students in my course on Exegetical Methods at Fuller Theological Seminary, Sacramento Campus, for their willingness to work through the chapters of this book in the fall of 2011: Katie Atkinson, Brandon Babcock, James Baird, Luke Chang, Corbett Cutts, Brandin Francabandera, Imre Golden, Robin Gordon, Brandon Hendricks, Brad Hickey, Nolan Hoyer, Richard Hultgren, Michael LaFarge and Erica Nestle. I am also grateful to Max Botner and Richard Rohlfing for technical and substantive assistance with this project in its final stages. I am also grateful to Amanda Y. Rodgers for help with formatting the manuscript and to Christian Amondson and the editorial team at Wipf and Stock for their expert and courteous assistance at every stage of the publication process. My wife, Kathy, kindly read through the manuscript and saved me from many errors of grammar and substance. Those that remain are my own.

Now, before you begin, set out a pen and paper, and a Bible (NRSV or NIV). By following the suggested exercises in each chapter, you will make the most efficient use of the material presented in the following pages. It is my hope that this book will provide a practical and enjoyable introduction to the use of the Old Testament in the New.

Abbreviations

BCE	Before the Common Era
BHS	*Biblia Hebraica Stuttgartensia*
CBQ	*Catholic Biblical Quarterly*
CE	Common Era
CEB	Common English Bible
CHB	*Cambridge History of the Bible*
CNTOT	*Commentary on the New Testament Use of the Old Testament*
DPL	*Dictionary of Paul and his Letters*
DSSE	*Dead Sea Scrolls in English* (Vermes)
DTIB	*Dictionary for Theological Interpretation of the Bible*
JBL	*Journal of Biblical Literature*
KJV	King James Version
LAB	*Liber Antiquitatum Biblicarum* (Pseudo-Philo)
LXX	Septuagint
MT	Masoretic Text
NA27	Nestle—Aland, *Novum Testamentum Graece*, 27th edition
NETS	*New English Translation of the Septuagint*
NIV	New International Version
NRSV	New Revised Standard Version
REB	Revised English Bible
RSV	Revised Standard Version
SBL	Society of Biblical Literature
UBS4	United Bible Societies Greek New Testament (Fourth Edition)

1

Form

THE STUDY OF THE Old Testament in the New Testament should begin with a careful observation of the passages as they appear in the two testaments. This is best done by comparing the New Testament text with that of the Hebrew (MT) and Greek (LXX) of the Old Testament. But even for those without a working knowledge of the original languages, the comparison of translations can provide a valuable introduction to the study. For example, if we set the NRSV version of Mark 1:3 alongside Isaiah 40:3 in the same translation we notice some interesting differences in text-form:

Isaiah 40:3	Mark 1:3
A voice cries out	The voice of one crying out in the
"In the wilderness prepare the	wilderness
way of the Lord	"Prepare the way of the Lord
Make straight in the desert a	Make his paths straight."
Highway for our God."	

There are several differences in this quotation from Isaiah 40 in Mark 1, but the one that you should especially notice is in the last line. Instead of "A highway for our God" in Isaiah, Mark reads, "Make his paths straight." We will return to the significance of this change in another chapter. Here we are simply alerted to this sort of change, and need to note that even seemingly small changes in wording can be important.

For another such change, look at the longest quotation from the Old Testament in Matthew, Matt 12:18: We compare the opening words of this verse with the text as it appears in the NIV:

Isaiah 42:1 (NIV)	Matthew 12:18(NIV)
Here is my servant whom I uphold	Here is my servant whom I have chosen
My chosen one in whom I delight	the one I love in whom I delight

You can spot several differences between the Old Testament text of Isaiah 42:1 and Matthew's version. But the one that jumps off the page is the change from "my chosen" to "the one whom I love."

Now look at the Septuagint (LXX), the Greek Old Testament:

> Isaiah 42:1 LXX (NETS)
> Jacob is my servant; I will lay hold of him;
> Israel is my chosen; my soul has accepted him.

ISAIAH 61 AND LUKE 4

Take another example of a clear quotation that involves a textual variation in the New Testament, a variation that I believe has important implications for exegesis, theology and ethics. Turn to Luke 4:18–19. Jesus read from the prophet Isaiah, chapter 61 in the synagogue at Nazareth. A comparison of the LXX and the printed text of Luke is interesting:

Isaiah 61:1–2	Luke 4:18–19
The spirit of the Lord God is	The Spirit of the Lord is
Upon me	upon me,
Because the Lord has	because the Lord has anointed me
Anointed me	to bring good news to the
He has sent me to bring good	poor.
News to the oppressed	He has sent me to proclaim
To bind up the brokenhearted	release to the captives
To proclaim liberty to the captives	and recovery of sight to the
And release to the prisoners	blind.

To proclaim the year of the Lord's favor And the day of vengeance of Our God;	to let the oppressed go free. to proclaim the year of the Lord's favor.

A careful study of the differences between Isaiah 61 and Luke 4 is instructive. In particular, notice that in Luke a line has been added ("To let the oppressed go free," which is taken from Isa 58:6) and a line has been omitted ("to heal the brokenhearted,"). The omitted line in the NRSV is found in the King James Version, and is the reading of the majority of New Testament manuscripts. However, most modern editors of the Greek New Testament do not think that Luke had the line. I disagree, and I think it belongs in the Gospel of Luke. It is difficult to imagine that Luke would have intentionally left out a reference to healing. [1]

PSALM 40 AND HEBREWS 10

The quotation from Isaiah 61 in Luke 4 gives us an example of a variation in the New Testament textual tradition, where the Old Testament text is secure. We next explore a quotation where the New Testament text is secure, and there is a variation in the Old Testament text, especially as regards the Greek version (LXX).

Turn to Heb 10:5, which quotes Ps 40:6:

Psalm 40:6 (NRSV)	Hebrews 10:5
Sacrifice and offering you did not desire	Sacrifices and offerings you have not desired,
but you have given me an open ear.	but a body you have prepared for me.

Notice that the NRSV, translating the MT, reads, "you have given me an open ear," whereas in Hebrews 10 the quotation takes the form "a body you have prepared for me." The writer of the Epistle to the Hebrews seems to be following the Greek Old Testament (LXX) which reads "a body you have prepared for me." At least this is the reading of manuscripts BSA of the Greek Old Testament (LXX).

---

1. Rodgers, *Text and Story*, 93–100.

But manuscripts G a follow the Hebrew in reading "but ears you have fashioned for me." (NETS)(ὠτία δὲ κατηρτίσω μοι).

So the manuscript tradition of the Greek Old Testament is divided, some following the Hebrew, but others having an alternative reading. Older commentators believed that Hebrews was following the LXX text, but more recent studies have suggested that the reading "a body" was the work of the author of Hebrews, and that the Christian manuscripts of the LXX, BSA, have been influenced by the text form found in the Epistle to the Hebrews. [2] In assessing the text form of Old Testament quotations it will be important not just to rely on our printed texts and translations, but also to keep an eye on any variant reading in both the the Old Testament and the New Testament textual traditions. This makes exploring the Old Testament in the New much more challenging, but also more interesting.

JOEL 2 AND ACTS 2

One of the best ways to explore and appreciate the textual differences in quotations of the Old Testament in the New Testament is to copy out the two texts by hand, and then to check your work. You may discover in the process that you have made some of the same mistakes in copying that the ancient Jewish and Christian scribes made when copying the scriptures. You might leave out a word or line. You might write the same word twice. Or you might substitute a well-known word for an obscure one. Try this experiment: Write out the text of Joel 2:28–32 from the NRSV or the NIV. Then from the same version you used for Joel, copy out along side of it the text of Acts 2:17–21. Underline or circle all differences, omissions or additions. Why do you think Luke has made the changes he has in reporting this quotation in Peter's Pentecost speech?

After you have done this exercise there is still more to do. The Acts of the Apostles is unique among New Testament books, in that its text has been transmitted from the earliest times in two distinct text-forms. There is the Alexandrian text form of Codex Vaticanus (B) which most scholars regard as the earliest and most

2. Jobes and Silva, *Invitation*, 195–197.

trustworthy. The other text is the so-called "Western" text, whose chief representative is Codex Bezae Cantabrigiensis (D). The D text (Bezae) is almost a tenth longer than the B (Vaticanus) text, and contains a number of colorful and edifying additions. Produced below is a synoptic form, in translation, of the two texts side by side for Acts 2:17–21

Codex Bezae (D)	*Codex Vaticanus (B)*
17. It shall be in the last days, says the Lord, I will pour out from my spirit On to all flesh and their sons and their Daughters shall prophesy and the young Men shall see visions and the old men Shall dream; 18. Both on my male Servants and on my female servants I Myself will pour out from my spirit; 19 And I will give wonders in heaven Above and signs on earth below; 20 the Sun turns into darkness and the moon Into blood before the great day of the Lord comes 21 and it shall be that Anyone who calls on the name of the Lord shall be rescued.	17 And it shall be after that, says God, I will pour out from my spirit on to all flesh and your sons and your daughters shall prophesy and your young men shall see visions and your old men shall dream dreams; 18 indeed, onto both my male servants and my female servants in those days I will pour out from my spirit and they shall prophesy. 19 And I will give wonders in heaven above and signs on earth below, blood and fire and clouds of smoke; 20 The sun shall be turned into Darkness and the moon into blood Before the great and glorious day Of the Lord comes 21 and it will be That everyone that calls on the Name of the Lord will be rescued.[3]

The first thing to notice is that the Alexandrian text (B) is somewhat longer than the "Western" text (D). This is strange, since the "Western" text, overall, is longer in Acts as we have noted. Now take the copy of the passage from Joel 2, which you have copied out and set it alongside these two versions of Acts. Better still, take the New English Translation of the Septuagint (NETS) and turn to p.802, column 2. (Note that the passage in LXX is Joel 2:28–32; the numbering is different from the MT). Note the differences carefully.

3. Ruis Camps and Read Heimerdinger, *Message*, 1, 165–66.

One rule among textual critics is that the shorter reading is usually original. Another rule commonly used by textual critics is that the passage that differs from the LXX is more likely to be original. It looks as though here the "Western" text (D) may be original. Of course, there is the possibility that both the B and the D text were written by Luke. Close observation of the text-form of the quotation raises some very interesting questions. Scholars have been wrestling with these issues, and offering various different solutions for generations.[4]

THE OLD TESTAMENT IN PAUL

In recent years there have been a number of studies on the use of the Old Testament in Paul. Perhaps the best place for the student to begin such a study is with the article on the Old Testament in Paul by Moises Silva in the *Dictionary of Paul and his Letters*. (DPL). On p. 631 of this dictionary you will find a chart of all the Old Testament citations in Paul. In this chart Silva gives five lists:

1. Paul agrees with both the MT and the LXX: 42 citations

2. Paul agrees with the MT against the LXX : 7 citations

3. Paul agrees with the LXX against the MT: 17 times

4. Paul's wording agrees with neither the LXX nor the MT : 31 citations

5. Debated instances : 10 times

It is clear that while Paul may have a slight preference for the LXX in his text form, he felt very much at liberty to use a form closer to the Hebrew (MT) if it suited the purposes of his argument. He also commonly quoted a form of the text that agrees with neither the Greek nor the Hebrew. This chart deserves careful study and will repay the effort. If you study the chart you will notice that Paul quotes from Deuteronomy 32 three times in Romans. It is clear that this passage, this so-called "Song of Moses," was very much in Paul's mind when he wrote the letter. But what is interesting to note is the

4. Metzger, *Textual Commentary*, 222–36.

text-form of the three different citations. In Rom 10:19 Paul quotes Deut 32:21:

> 19. Again I ask, did Israel not understand? First Moses says,
> "I will make you jealous of those
> Who are not a nation;
> With a foolish nation I will make you angry."

According to Silva's chart Paul is quoting this verse from Deuteronomy 32 in a form that agrees with both the Hebrew and the LXX. But Verse 35 from the same poem is quoted in Rom 12:19:

> 19. Beloved, never avenge yourselves, but leave room for
> the wrath of God;
> for it is written, "Vengeance is mine, I will repay, says
> the Lord."

In this quotation Paul agrees with the MT against the LXX. And if we turn to Rom 15:10, the third time Paul quotes from this passage, we find that his text form agrees with the LXX against the MT. The citation from Deut 32:43, in Paul's combination of several quotations from the scripture about the Gentiles and Jews praising God together, reads:

And again he says,
"Rejoice, O Gentiles, with his people."

The exact wording of the quotations from Deuteronomy 32 was a matter of considerable debate in the time of Paul, and the differences between the Hebrew and Greek versions were theologically significant. We will pursue this topic further in Chapter 6 on the history of interpretation. But it is important to note here the variety of text form in Paul's scripture citations.

One other large category (31 instances) in Silva's chart is the scripture citations in Paul where his text-form agrees with neither the LXX nor the MT. In these places Paul seems to be quoting from another source. Look, for example, at Eph 4:8, and set it alongside the NRSV of Ps 68:18. The form of Paul's quotation is very interesting:

Psa. 68:18 NRSV	Eph 4:8
You ascended the high mount,	When he ascended on high he

| Leading captives in your train | made captivity itself a captive; |
| And receiving gifts from people. | he gave gifts to his people. |

Note that whereas the Psalm reads "receiving gifts," Ephesians reads "he gave gifts." The NRSV of Ps 68:19 represents the reading of both the MT and the LXX. So Paul's form of the quotation differs from both. Those puzzled by the fact that Paul "misquotes" both the Hebrew and the Greek will turn to the commentaries and find that "he gave gifts" (ἔδωκεν δόματα) corresponds to the reading of the Targum of the psalm. The *targums* were Aramaic translations or paraphrases of the Old Testament, which translated the scriptures into Aramaic for those who could not understand Hebrew. These targums often incorporated interpretation as well as translation. So this may explain the source of the text-form of Paul's quotation. The text in this form serves well the point that Paul is making in this section of Ephesians, which concerns the gifts God has given to the church.

HABAKKUK 2:4 IN THE NEW TESTAMENT

One final quotation that we will consider in analyzing the text-form of the Old Testament in the New is Hab 2:4 as it appears in Rom 1:17, Gal 3:11 and Heb 10:38. This is a fascinating, and complicated case, illustrating how important it is to keep our eyes on the variations in both the New Testament and the Old Testament texts. We begin with Gal 3:11, and note that the familiar King James Version "the just shall live by faith" is found in both the Galatians and Habakkuk. This is also the form of the quotation in the KJV for both Rom 1:17 and Heb 10:38. Now look at the NIV and compare Hab 2:4 and the New Testament quotations:

> Hab 2:4 But the righteous will live by his faith.
> Rom 1:17 The righteous will live by faith.
> Gal 3:11 The righteous will live by faith.
> Heb 10:38 But my righteous one will live by faith.

Note that the text form in Paul is different from either Habakkuk (his faith) or Hebrews (my righteous one). Observe also that the NIV has a footnote at Heb 10:38 which reads "One early manuscript *But the righteous.*" This manuscript is papyrus P13, which dates to the late third or early fourth century. But this is not the whole story at Heb10:38. Another early manuscript (D, Claromontanus, 6th century) reads not "my righteous one" but "by my faith." If we turn to the LXX of Hab 2:4 we find that the manuscript tradition of the LXX also has all three readings, as well as a reading corresponding to the MT "by his faith." This is the reading of the Greek Minor Prophets Scroll from Nahal Hever (8HevXIIgr). It is clear that the text form of this quotation in both the Old and New Testaments is more complicated than it appears from a simple comparison of our printed texts and translation. A thorough study of the text-form of quotations from the Old Testament in the New Testament will consider the range of textual variations, in order to determine which form in each testament was original, but also to understand why the alternative readings arose. And this is especially important for a text like Hab 2:4, whose use by the New Testament writers is theologically significant. In many instances these variations will be discussed in the larger critical commentaries on the New Testament, and should be studied carefully. Both the text-form and the textual variety of these quotations offer us what C.H. Dodd called "the substructure of New Testament Theology."[5]

FOR FURTHER EXPLORATION

There is no better way to appreciate the importance of the text-form for the study of quotations of the Old Testament in the New Testament than to copy out, either in English or (better still) in Greek the text-form of larger quotations and set the Old and New Testaments side-by-side. Here are some important longer quotations for such an exploration:

> Matthew 4:14–16 = Isaiah 9:1–2
> Matthew 13:13–15 = Isaiah 6:9–10
> Acts 2:25–28 = Psalm 16:8–11
> Hebrews 1:10–12 = Psalm 102:25–27

5. Dodd, *Scriptures,* subtitle

Hebrews 8:8–12 (10:16–17) = Jeremiah 31:31–34

Other long quotations can be spotted easily by thumbing through the United Bible Societies Greek New Testament and noticing larger indented sections in bold type. This exercise will be very helpful to anyone who wishes to understand the nature of the biblical text. Such a direct encounter with the text can at first be upsetting to some students since it appears that the New Testament writer may be "misquoting" the Old Testament. But in fact it can open up for the student a whole new appreciation of the disciplined freedom with which the New Testament writers handled the sacred text. It can also lead to a deeper appreciation of the Bible as both human word and holy Scripture.

2

Introduction

By the term "Introduction," I am referring to the way an Old Testament text is introduced by a New Testament writer. There are basically two types of citations: 1) Quotations with an introductory formula. 2) Allusions and echoes without any formula of introduction.

QUOTATIONS WITH AN INTRODUCTORY FORMULA

Many of the quotations from the Old Testament in the New Testament are preceded by an introductory formula. In the Gospel of Matthew we read the words "All this took place to fulfill what had been spoken by the Lord through the prophet. . . . " (1:23). Similar wording introduces eleven other quotations in Matthew's Gospel. St Paul uses the phrase "as it is written" to introduce a number of his quotations. Look at the formulae introducing Paul's quotations in Rom 1:17, 9:33 and 11:25. Note the variety of formulae introducing the string of quotations in Rom 15:9–12. Other New Testament writers follow the same convention. 1 Pet 2:6 reads, "for it stands in scripture." The Epistle to the Hebrews has a number of interesting formulae introducing quotations from the scriptures of Israel. In 3:7, for example, the author introduces a long quotation from Psalm 95 with the words,

"Therefore, as the Holy Spirit says." In Heb 2:6 the writer introduces a quotation from Psalm 8 with the words, "But someone has testified somewhere." Was the writer in too much of a hurry, or not in possession of a Psalms scroll, or could he or she not remember which Psalm it was?

Sometimes a New Testament writer names a particular Old Testament author, in an introductory formula. Here are some examples:

> John 12:38: This was to fulfill the word spoken by the Prophet Isaiah.
> Acts 1:20: For it is written in the second Psalm.
> Acts 28:25: The Holy Spirit was right in saying to your ancestors through the prophet Isaiah. . .
> Romans 9:25: As indeed he says in Hosea,
> Romans 10:20: Then Isaiah is so bold as to say,

Occasionally the New Testament writer seems to attribute a quotation to the wrong Old Testament writer. For example, in Mark 1:2 the evangelist writes, "As it is written in the prophet Isaiah." He then launches into a quotation from Malachi! (This is followed by a quotation from Isaiah 40). Scholars have offered a variety of explanations for this curious phenomenon. Some have suggested a "testimony book" hypothesis to explain this: a collection of Old Testament texts that were drawn together for Christian preaching, teaching and apologetic. Others think that Isaiah was cited because his words point to a key theme of the Gospel of Mark, "The Way of the Lord." It is interesting to note that many manuscripts correct the "error" by changing the wording in the introductory formula to "in the prophets." We will return to this interesting problem later in the book.

The New Testament writers are conscious that they are quoting the words of human authors of the Old Testament books. But they are also aware, as some of the formulae make clear, that the words express the divine voice. This will be especially evident where the voice is identified in the formulae as the Holy Spirit. (Acts 28:25, Heb 3:7). In these formulae the writer makes it clear that he is citing the inspired and authoritative word of God. This is also evident in formulae like "For the Lord has commanded us saying," (Acts 13:47) a formula that introduces a quotation from Isa 49:6. These formulae clearly demonstrate that the authors believe the books they are quoting to be the word of God.

ALLUSIONS AND ECHOES OF SCRIPTURE WITHOUT AN INTRODUCTORY FORMULA

There are a number of places in the New Testament where an Old Testament passage is cited extensively, but without any recognition that Scripture is being cited. Look at 1 Pet 2:21–25 in the United Bible Societies Greek New Testament, where a number of phrases from Isaiah 53 are embedded in the writer's reflection on the suffering of Christ. The Old Testament phrases are in bold type. Because of this, the allusions are easy to spot even if you do not know any Greek.

These allusions to the fourth Servant Song (Isa 52:13—53:12) are helpfully laid out in tabular form (in English) in Karen Jobes' Commentary on 1 Peter [1]

In a similar way, Paul incorporates a number of phrases from the Old Testament in his song of praise to God's wisdom at the end of Romans 11:33–36. Can you find the quoted words and the place they come from in the Old Testament? For clues, look at a good cross-reference Bible.

> 33 O the depth of the riches and wisdom and knowledge of God!
> How unsearchable are his judgments and how inscrutable his ways!
> 34 "For who has known the mind of the Lord?
> Or who has been his Counselor?"

1. Jobes, *1 Peter*, 194.

> 35 Or who has given a gift to him,
> to receive a gift in return?"
> 36 For from him and through him and to him are all things
> To him be glory forever. Amen.

These longer allusions to the Old Testament are fairly easy to recognize, and it is likely that the early Christian writer and reader alike would recognize them as citations from Scripture. But there are some places where scholars have detected echoes of the Old Testament in the New Testament writings, where just one phrase, or even a word, may indicate a much larger passage or narrative from the scriptures of Israel. Here is an important, and theologically significant example. Turn to Mark 1:11 (or its parallels in Matt 3:17 and Luke 3:22). The wording in each is similar but not identical. How many Old Testament echoes can you spot? Many scholars believe that as many as three Old Testament texts are echoed in the voice from heaven at the baptism of Jesus (Psalm 2, Isaiah 42 and Genesis 22). The words "You are my son" are an echo of Psa 2:7. The expression "in you I am well-pleased" looks back to Isaiah 42, the opening description of the Servant of the Lord. The word "beloved" (perhaps better translated "only") reflects the story of the near sacrifice of Isaac in Genesis 22: "Take your son, your only son, whom you love, and go to the land of Moriah, and offer him there as a burnt offering. . . ." The presence of some of these echoes in the voice at the baptism is debated, but there is an increasing recognition among scholars that all three passages are echoed.[2] Here are the proposed echoes in Mark 1:11 and parallels in tabular form:

> You are my Son —Psa 2:7
> The Beloved —Gen 22:1
> With you I am well pleased —Isa 42:1

These echoes of the Scriptures of Israel in the New Testament are not introduced with any formula because often the word or phrase is so familiar to writer and reader alike that no introductory formula is needed. This is a common feature of literature in any culture. For example, in any speech or essay in contemporary

2. Green, *Luke*, 186–87.

America one can use the expressions "Pearl Harbor," or "Watergate" or "9/11" without having to give any explanation such as, "By 'Watergate' I mean the political scandal in which the Nixon administration spied on the headquarters of the Democratic party in the Watergate hotel, and then lied about its involvement. The scandal eventually led to the resignation of President Richard M. Nixon." No American needs such an explanation. The story is so widely known and deeply imbedded in our cultural consciousness that the mere mention of the word "Watergate" evokes the whole incident. Similarly, the first readers or hearers of the gospel story needed only to hear the word "beloved" (ἀγαπητός) to think of the story of the "Akedah" or "binding" of Isaac. (Genesis 22)

Another example is in the story of Jesus' Transfiguration. In Luke's account of the story there is the additional information that Moses and Elijah appeared with Jesus and were "speaking of his departure, which he was about to accomplish at Jerusalem," (Luke 9:31). The word used for "departure" is "exodus" (ἔξοδον). This one word would evoke for any Jewish reader the great story of the exodus, God's deliverance of the people of Israel out of Egypt, as told in the book by that name. One word evokes a whole story, and indicates that the death and resurrection of Jesus is the new exodus of the people of God.

IDENTIFYING ECHOES OF THE OLD TESTAMENT IN THE NEW TESTAMENT

The pioneering work on echoes of the Old Testament in the New Testament was done by Richard B. Hays in his 1989 book *Echoes of Scripture in the Letters of Paul*. Hays outlined a number of criteria for recognizing echoes of Scripture in the New Testament, and these have proved both fruitful and controversial. Hays proposed the following seven tests to determine Inter-textual echoes:[3]

Availability. Was the proposed source of the echo available to the author and/or original readers?

3. Hays, *Echoes*, 29–32.

Volume: The volume of an echo is determined primarily by the degree of explicit repetition of words or syntactical patterns, but other factors may also be relevant: How distinctive or prominent is the precursor text within Scripture, and how much rhetorical stress does the echo receive in the New Testament writing?

Recurrence: How often does the New Testament writer cite or allude to the same scriptural passage, or its broader context in the Old Testament?

Thematic Coherence: How well does the alleged echo fit into the line of argument that the New Testament writer is developing?

Historical Plausibility: Could the New Testament writer have intended the alleged meaning effect? Could the readers have understood it?

History of Interpretation: Have other readers, both critical and pre-critical, heard the same echoes?

Satisfaction: With or without clear confirmation from the other criteria listed here, does the proposed reading make sense? Does it illuminate the surrounding discourse? Does it produce for the reader a satisfying account of the effect of the inter-textual relation?

These seven criteria for identifying echoes of Scripture in the New Testament, developed by Richard Hays for his exploration of inter-textuality in Paul, have been adapted here so as to apply to the whole New Testament. Hays has not been without his critics. Nevertheless, many scholars have found Hays' approach a real advance in understanding the varied use of the Old Testament in the New.

To explore the presence of echoes of scripture in the New Testament documents, try this experiment. Look at 1 Pet1:13–20. Many scholars believe that the story of the Passover/Exodus is echoed in this passage. The formula quotation from Lev 19:2 is certainly taken from the broader story of the Exodus and wilderness wanderings. What other echoes of the Passover/Exodus story can you find in this short passage?

Scholars believe that the Exodus story is echoed elsewhere in the New Testament. We have already seen this echo of Exodus in the case of the Transfiguration account in Luke 9:31. Silvia Keesmaat has argued that the theme of Exodus has shaped the argument of Romans. 8[4] Read over Rom 8:14–24. Can you find any language or themes in this passage that reflect the Exodus story?

Now turn to the Mark 12:1–12, Jesus parable of the Wicked Tenants. Note that Jesus follows the parable in verse 10 with a formula quotation, from Psa18:22: "Have you not read the scripture: 'The stone that the builders rejected has become the cornerstone; this is the Lord's doing, and it is amazing in our eyes.'" But the parable in verses 1–9 is a clear echo of an Old Testament parable, "The Song of the Unfruitful Vineyard" in Isa 5:1–7. Read over this parable in Isaiah, and discover for yourself how Jesus applies it to his own ministry. In the words of N.T.Wright, here is *"The story of Jesus telling the Story of Israel,"*[5] Jesus is putting his impending death and Resurrection at the center of that story. But Mark does not need to remind the reader that the parable of the Wicked Tenants is a rewrite of the old parable from Isaiah 5. His earliest readers already know that. The story from their scriptures is imbedded in their culture, and part of their mental furniture.

It is clear from the above observations that while an introductory formula may indeed alert the reader to the divine authority of the scripture being quoted, the *absence* of such a formula in connection with a reference from the Scriptures of Israel may be as important as its presence. It indicates that there is a shared thought world between writer and readers. Because of that common culture of confidence in the sacred text, and familiarity with it, no formula of introduction is needed. One word may be all that is required to evoke a whole story.

In his study of biblical inter-textuality, Richard Hays has argued that the portion of an Old Testament passage, quoted or alluded to in the New Testament evokes the wider context. In Hays' words, the cited portion is "merely the tip of the iceberg." These explicit words " point to a larger mass just under the surface." [6] This technique of citing a word or phrase to evoke a whole passage was described by Quintillian among ancient writers and widely

4. Keesmatt, *Paul*; Wright, *Paul*, 98, 178.
5. Wright, *New Testament*, 394. Italics his.
6. Hays, *Conversion*, 27.

practiced by writers both ancient and modern.[7] This technique is called *metalepsis*. Hays asserts, "When a literary echo links the text in which it occurs to an earlier text, the figurative effect of the echo can lie in the unstated or suppressed (transumed) points of resonance between the two texts." [8] One of the assumptions behind Hays' assertion is that the writer will have intended and the readers will have heard the echo, and be aware of the wider context of the quoted material. It is rather like in our age of widespread internet use, where a hyperlink or icon on a computer can give access to a whole mass of information within.

Some have questioned this assumption. Christopher Stanley, for example, contends those in Paul's churches for whom his letters were intended were likely illiterate and would not hear the echo or recognize its broader context.[9] The whole matter of reader competence and ancient literacy is complicated, and Stanley's criticisms need to be carefully considered. [10]But many have continued to find Hay's "metaleptic" approach to intertextuality both satisfying and fruitful. Studies such as Joel Marcus' *The Way of the Lord*, Rikki E. Watts' *Isaiah's New Exodus in Mark*, and J. Ross Wagner's *Heralds of Good News*, (To name just a few important works) bear witness to the continuing appeal of this approach.

Now look at an example, Jesus' cry from the cross in Mark 15:34 (with a parallel in Matt 27:46). In this cry, Jesus is presented by Mark and Matthew as quoting from the opening verse of Psalm 22:

"My God, my God, why have you forsaken me?"

Recently Holly J. Carey conducted a study of this allusion to Psalm 22 in its cultural and Markan context and concluded that in citing the one verse Mark had the whole Psalm in mind. The fact that it is the opening verse of the Psalm, that the Psalm is alluded to elsewhere in Mark's passion Narrative, and that it was understood

7. Quintillian, *Institutes of Oratory*, 8.6.
8. Hays, *Echoes*, 20.
9. Stanley, *As it is Written*, 132.
10. See 82

as a "Psalm of the Righteous Sufferer" in the Judaism of the Second Temple period supports her conclusion that Mark is referring to the whole Psalm and not just to the first verse. [11] Psalm 22, its story and shape, undergirds the whole Markan passion-resurrection narrative, even though its wording surfaces in only a few places.

Here is an example of proposed *metalepsis* that you can investigate for yourself. Some scholars suggest that Paul is especially focused on Isaiah 40–55 in Romans. See, for example, J. Ross Wagner's large study *Heralds of Good News: Isaiah and Paul "in Concert" in the Letter to the Romans.* Wagner observed that Paul seems not just to be quoting isolated verses from Isaiah, but is conscious of the whole passage, i.e. he is "In Concert" with the story Isaiah is telling as he wrestles with God's dealings with Israel in the light Christ's life, death and resurrection. Look through Romans 9–11 and see how many quotations and allusions you can find from the book of Isaiah (especially chapters 40–55). This is a fairly simple exercise for anyone with access to a good study Bible with cross—references. Does it seem to you that Paul is especially conscious of this section of the Scriptures of Israel at this point?

A similar fruitful exercise can be conducted by reading 1 Peter. Read through the letter and see how many references you can find to Psalm 34. The allusions in 1 Pet 2:2 and 3:10–12 are easy to spot. But there may be several more references to the psalm in the letter. Karen Jobes lists no less than 7 other allusions or echoes of Psalm 34 in 1 Peter, and some scholars claim to have found more. [12] See which ones you can spot. It looks like Peter had the whole Psalm in mind as he wrote his letter to the Christians in Asia Minor.

In this chapter we have reviewed a number of Old Testament quotations in the New Testament, which are introduced with an introductory formula. Many of these formulae make it clear that the New Testament writer regards the text he is quoting as the word of God. But a number of Old Testament allusions and echoes have no formula marking them out as Scripture. These too are significant since the absence of a formula may indicate a shared culture and

---

11. Carey, *Cry passim.*

12. Jobes, *1 Peter*, 221–23.

assumptions between writer and reader. One word or phrase can serve, in the words of Richard Hays, to "activate Israel's canonical memory."[13]

FOR FURTHER EXPLORATION

Paul's letter to the Philippians contains no quotations from the Old Testament introduced with a formula like "as it is written. . . " But that does not mean that Paul is not referring to the scriptures of Israel in the letter. Scholars have discerned a number of Old Testament echoes in the letter. Take Paul's famous "Hymn to Christ" in Phil 2:5–11 and see how many allusions or echoes of the Old Testament you can find in this passage. Then check your discovery with a Bible that gives cross-references. If nothing comes to mind, look at Rom 14:11. See also *CNTOT,* 836–838. It is generally agreed that there is at least one allusion to the Old Testament in this hymn, and there may well be more.

13. Hays, *Echoes,* 51.

3

Selection

WHEN I WAS A graduate student, my special area of study was the use of the Old Testament in 1 Peter. One of the questions that fascinated me then, and continues to intrigue me now, is why did this author choose these particular Old Testament texts in writing to persecuted Christians in Asia Minor? What was the principle (or principles) governing the selection of these texts? Is there a discernible theme, idea or agenda that draws them together?

My study made it clear that the three Old Testament texts quoted in 1 Pet 2:6–8 were drawn together by a common word, in this case the word "stone" (λίθος):

> 6. For it stands in Scripture:
> "See, I am laying in Zion a stone (λίθος):
> A cornerstone chosen and precious;
> And whoever believes in him
> Will not be put to shame." (Isa. 28:16)
> 7. To you then who believe, he is precious; but for those who do not believe,
> "The stone (λίθος): that the builders rejected
> Has become the very head of the corner" (Psa 118:22)
> 8. And
> "A stone (λίθος) that makes them stumble,

and a rock that makes them fall." (Isa 8:14)
They stumbled because they disobeyed the word,
As they were destined to do.

All three of the Old Testament texts quoted in this passage have the word "stone" in them, and this key word served to unite them together in early Christian thinking, teaching and preaching. It is interesting to notice that the author of First Peter is here following a Jewish principle of interpretation, common at the time, called *Gezera shawah*, where one passage may be explained by another if they contain similar words or phrases. [1]

Also I noticed that there are at least two places in 1 Peter, 2:2 and 3:10–12, where the writer quotes from Psalm 34. Others have studied the influence of Psalm 34 on 1 Peter and have noted at least seven places where there are likely to be allusions to Psalm 34 in 1 Peter.[2] Clearly, this Psalm was important for the author of 1 Peter.

Nevertheless, the reason why other Old Testament texts were chosen was not obvious to me. I failed, for example, to see why the quotation from Isaiah 40: 6–8, quoted at length in 1:24–25, should have suggested itself to the writer of the letter. Since then it has struck me that the theme of Exile, which is very much at the heart of the letter (1:1, 2:11), is also the background of Isaiah 40, from which these verses are taken. But I still was in search of some overarching principle, or principles, that would explain the selection of these particular passages by 1 Peter.

It was then that I read 4 Maccabees 18:10–19, a passage at the very end of a document from about the same time as the writing of the New Testament (though independent of it) that cited some of the same Old Testament passages that were important to 1 Peter (which is itself written to Jewish Christians faced with persecution for their faith). See if you can discover some of these passages as you read through this moving tribute of a mother to her sons, who have just been put to death for their faithfulness to the law of God. The mother is recounting the scripture passages that the father taught his children:

1. Evans, "Jewish Exegesis," 382.
2. Jobes, *1 Peter*, 221–222.

10. While he was still with you, he taught you the law and the prophets. 11 He read to you about Abel slain by Cain, and Isaac who was offered as a burnt offering, and about Joseph in prison. 12 He told you of the zeal of Phinehas, and he taught you about Hananiah, Azariah and Mishael in the fire. 13 He praised Daniel in the den of lions and blessed him. 14 He reminded you of the scripture of Isaiah, which says, "Even though you go through the fire, the flame shall not consume you." 15 He sang to you the songs of the Psalmist David, who said, "Many are the afflictions of the righteous." 16 He recounted to you Solomon's proverb, "There is a tree of life for those who do his will." 17 He confirmed the query of, Ezekiel "Shall these bones live?" 18 For he did not forget to teach you the song that Moses taught, which says, 19 "I kill and I make alive: this is your life and the length of your days." (NRSV)

The writers of 1 Peter and of 4 Maccabees, though completely independent, both share the same concern (encouraging God's people who are being persecuted for their faith), and both seem to be drawing on the same scripture passages which were especially valued by those suffering trials for their faith in Second Temple Judaism. (Psalm 34, Proverbs 3, and possibly also Genesis 22).

C.H. DODD

There seem to be a number of Old Testament passages which the New Testament writers especially turned to when seeking to understand, proclaim or defend their conviction about Jesus the Messiah. The pioneering work on this matter of the selection of Old Testament passages was C.H. Dodd's *According to the Scriptures*. This short volume, originally given as lectures at Princeton in 1950, is really the keynote for the modern study of the Old Testament in the New. Dodd notes that there were 15 passages from the scriptures to which the New Testament writers returned again and again as *testimonia* to the gospel facts. By focusing on these *testimonia*, Dodd proposed, "What we are trying to do is to get an opening into the intellectual workshop of the early Church, and to watch its mind at work."[3] He was claiming to unearth "The substructure of New Testament theology" (to quote the subtitle of his book).

PSALM 2:7

Let us explore some of these texts, cited often and by more than one New Testament author. Pride of place in Dodd's list is given to Psa 2:7: "You are my son; today I have begotten you." This verse is cited, with the introductory formula: "as also it is written in the second psalm" in Paul's speech in Pisidian Antioch in Acts 13:33. At Heb 1:5, and again at Heb 5:5, Psa 2:7 is quoted, with a formula indicating that it is God who is speaking, as a testimony to the divine sonship of Jesus. Dodd notes that this text is probably to be recognized behind the voice at the baptism of Jesus, and at his transfiguration. (Mark 1:11, Matt 3:17, Luke 3: 22; Mark 9:7, Matt 17:5, Luke 9:35). Indeed, in St. Luke's account of the voice at the baptism, some manuscripts (D etc.) give the wording of the voice exactly as in Psa 2:7. Although I do not think this is what Luke originally wrote, it shows that scribes clearly heard the echo of Psa 2: 7 in the voice at the baptism of Jesus.

What we see here is that several New Testament writers understand Psalm 2:7 as an important scriptural witness to Jesus' divine sonship. It indicates a widespread early Christian assumption that this psalm was especially valuable in offering scriptural support to their conviction that Jesus was the Son of God.

THE SUFFERING SERVANT

Another Old Testament passage cited by several New Testament writers is the fourth Servant Song, Isa 52:13—53:12 (here referred to for convenience as Isaiah 53). We note that Matthew cites Isa 53:4, using his customary fulfillment formula, to show that scripture is fulfilled in the healing ministry of Jesus: "This was to fulfill what had been spoken through the prophet Isaiah, 'He took our

3. Dodd, *Scriptures*, 28.

infirmities and bore our diseases" (Matt 8:17). Luke cites Isa 53:12, presenting Jesus as understanding the verse as a prediction of his arrest, "For I tell you, this scripture must be fulfilled in me, 'And he was counted among the lawless.'" (Luke 22:37, see also the variant reading at Mark 15:28). In Acts 8:32–33, the Ethiopian Eunuch is reading Isaiah 53, and Acts cites Isa 53:7–8 *in extenso*. Luke continues the story with the Eunuch's question, "About whom, may I ask you, does the prophet say this, about himself or about someone else?" The story continues in Acts 8:35, "Then Philip began to speak, and starting with this scripture, he proclaimed to him the good news about Jesus." A third place where we find Isaiah 53 cited is in 1 Pet 2:21–25, a passage we have already considered. Peter weaves a number of phrases from Isaiah 53 into his description of Jesus' suffering and death. There is no introductory formula, for writer and readers alike will know the passage as one of the most fruitful for showing how the Messiah must suffer, according to the scriptures.

Professor Morna Hooker is famously skeptical about the importance of Isaiah 53 in the New Testament. Yet she is convinced that at least at Rom 4:25 Paul is alluding to this passage when he writes that Jesus " was handed over to death for our trespasses and was raised for our justification."[4] Paul also cites Isaiah 53:1 at Rom 10:16, and John cites the same verse in John 12:38, "Lord, who has believed our message, and to whom has the arm of the Lord been revealed?" Dodd wrote,

> That Paul had read the Fourth Gospel is impossible, and that the Fourth Evangelist had read the Epistle to the Romans would be a conjecture For which no evidence can be adduced. It is a reasonable inference that Both writers employed a *testimonium* already recognized. [5]

It is clear from this brief survey of quotations and clear allusions to Isaiah 53 in the New Testament (we have not even treated echoes such as Mark 10:45) that Matthew, Luke, John, Paul, and Peter all agree in selecting Isaiah 53 as scriptural witness to Jesus. The

---

4. Hooker, "Did Jesus Use Isaiah 53," 101.

5. Dodd, *Scriptures*, 39.

Gospel writers also point to Jesus as the one who originally applied the fourth Servant Song of Isaiah to his mission.

PSALM 110:1

The most frequently quoted Old Testament text in the New Testament is Psa 110:1, "The Lord says to my lord, 'Sit at my right hand until I make your enemies your footstool." Multiple New Testament writers quote or allude to this text. Most of them are listed in the back of the United Bible Societies' Greek New Testament in the index of quotations and the index of allusions and verbal parallels. In his classic study of Psalm 110 in Early Christianity, *Glory at the Right Hand*, David M. Hay gives a comprehensive list of quotations and allusions to Psalm 110:1 in the New Testament and other early Christian writings. If you look these passages up, and even copy them out, you will get a sense of how important this psalm was for the earliest Christians. Again, the Gospel writers represent Jesus as the first person in the Christian movement to point to this text as a fruitful messianic *testimonium*.

Here is David M. Hay's list of New Testament references to Psalm 110:1 for your study and exploration: Matt. 22:44, Matt 26:64, Mark 12:36, Mark 14:64, "Mark" 16:19, Luke 20:42–43, Luke 22:69, Acts 2:33, Acts 2:34–36, Acts 5:31, Acts 7:55–56, Rom 8:34, 1 Cor 15:25, Eph 1:20, Eph 2:6, Col 3:1, Heb 1:3, Heb 1:13, Heb 8:1, Heb 10:12–13, Heb 12:2, 1 Pet 3:22, Rev 3:12. The ambitious student may want to explore the references to this verse in other early Christian writings: 1 Clem 36:5, Polycarp, Philippians 2:1, Barnabas 12:10 Apocalypse of Peter 6, Sibiline Oracle 2.243, Apocrophon of James 14:30, Hegesippus (Eusebius EH 2.23.13).[6] A convenient list of citations of the Old Testament in the New may be found in the appendix of the two commonly used Greek New Testaments, The United Bible Societies fourth edition and the Nestle-Aland twenty-seventh edition.[7] The student would find it a valuable exercise to

---

6. Hay, *Glory*, 163–65.

7. *UBS4*, 887–901, *NA27*, 770–806.

copy out from the NRSV in parallel columns any one of the texts listed below in both Old Testament and New Testament forms.

The following is C.H. Dodd's list of the 15 Old Testament passages that were especially important to the New Testament writers. I urge you to look these up and write out the verses in the space provided.

Psalm 2:7
Psalm 8:4–6
Psalm 110:1
Psalm 118:22–23
Isaiah 6:9–10
Isaiah 53:1
Isaiah 40:3–5
Isaiah 28:16
Genesis 12:2
Jeremiah 31:31–34
Joel 2:28–32
Zechariah 9:9
Habakkuk 2:4
Isaiah 61:1–2
Deuteronomy 18:15, 19.

We have already explored the use of three of these texts by multiple New Testament writers: Psa 2:7, Isaiah 53 and Psa 110:1. A valuable next step would be to take one or more of the texts among the 15 that have not been discussed, and discover which New Testament writers make use of them. Ask yourself the question: what was it that attracted the earliest Christians to these particular scripture texts?

THE TEXT AND THE CONTEXT

In his groundbreaking study, Dodd went on to propose that when a text from the Old Testament was quoted by a New Testament author, it was not simply lifted from its context and applied to the new Christian situation. Rather, he asserted that the early Christians cited texts with the wider context in mind. Rather than quoting single isolated proof-texts, the New Testament writers considered the Old Testament passages from which they came. Dodd asserts that the sections of scripture from which the phrase or verse was taken "were understood as *wholes*, and particular verses or sentences were quoted from them rather as pointers to the whole context than as constituting testimonies in and for themselves."[8] He gives evidence for this contention in Chapter III of *According to the Scriptures*. This view, that Christians had whole passages in mind, even when quoting only a small fragment, and that they paid attention to the context from which their quotations and allusions were drawn has been criticized by some. For example, Don Juel asserted that "Christian interpreters, like their Jewish contemporaries, were capable of abstracting a verse or a sentence from its literary context to make a point or to discover a new truth in it. [9] Thus E. Käsemann wrote concerning Paul's use of Hos 1:10 in Rom 9:29, "As is his custom Paul understands the sayings as eschatological oracles without considering their original sense."[10]

But the majority view remains that early Christian exegesis was not atomistic (quoting individual words out of context) but contextual.[11] Each student of the Old Testament in the New must decide for herself or himself whether Mark or John or Paul is using the Old Testament merely as a "grab-bag of isolated oracles"[12] or whether they are conscious of the plot or story from which these texts are taken. My own view is the latter. The New Testament writers normally display an awareness and sensitivity to the context of the Old Testament quotations, although that awareness is colored by their conviction that this story has reached its climax in Jesus the Messiah. The best way for the student to decide on this issue is to read through the third chapter of Dodd's *According to the Scriptures*, entitled "The Bible of the Early Church." Here Dodd organizes these often cited scripture passages under four headings:

8. Dodd, *Scriptures*, 126.

9. Juel, *Messianic Exegesis*, 21

10. Käsemann, *Romans*, 274.

11. Carey, *Cry, passim*.

12. Hays, *Conversion*, 48.

1) Apocalyptic-eschatological Scriptures. 2) Scriptures of the New Israel. 3) Scriptures of the servant of the Lord and the Righteous Sufferer. 4) Unclassified Scriptures.

Since Dodd's seminal work was published in 1952, many scholars have explored the use of the Old Testament in the New in order to clarify the principles that led to the selection of certain passages. Perhaps no study has been more influential than Richard Hays' *Echoes of Scripture in the Letters of Paul*. Hays drew attention to the way in which even a word or phrase in a letter of Paul could evoke a larger passage or story from the Old Testament. Subsequent to Hays' work several important studies have served to show how whole sections of the Old Testament have shaped the thought and language of the New Testament writers. This is especially the case with regard to Isaiah 40–55. Joel Marcus' study *The Way of the Lord* (1992) and Rikki E. Watts' *Isaiah's New Exodus in Mark* (2000) have added new dimension to our understanding of Mark's use of the Old Testament. J. Ross Wagner's *Heralds of Good News: Isaiah and Paul In Concert in the Letter to the Romans* (2002) gives some indication in the very title that Paul is respecting the context, indeed retelling the story, of Isaiah 40–55. To put it provocatively, it is not so much Paul selecting Isaiah as Isaiah selecting Paul.

HABAKKUK 2:4 AND ROMANS 1:17

Half a century ago, in 1962, I made my first discovery of this kind while memorizing the Epistle to the Romans. As I thought about Paul's key quotation from Hab 2:4 in Rom 1:17, it struck me that the broader question Paul was addressing in the early chapters of the letter (indeed throughout Romans) was one of theodicy, i.e. "What should we say? That God is unrighteous to inflict wrath on us?" (Rom 3:5). Then I noticed that this was precisely the same question that Habakkuk is asking in chapter 1, a question which climaxes in the affirmation in Hab 2:4 "the Righteous will live by his faith" (NIV).

The view I state here has not gone unchallenged. For example, Christopher Stanley asserts that in Rom 1:17 Paul disregarded the context of Hab 2:4 when he adapted the verse as the motto of his gospel.[13] But my observation that Habakkuk and Paul are wrestling with the same question (Is God unjust?) puts a different spin on the issue. Richard Hays seemed to have the more penetrating analysis of Paul's use of Habakkuk when he stated:

> In Habakkuk, the passage that Paul quotes comes as the nub of God's answer to the prophet's complaint (Hab 1:2) against the apparent injustice of God . . .Thus when Paul quotes Hab 2:4 we cannot help hearing the echoes—unless we are tone-deaf—of Habakkuk's theodicy question.[14]

There are many such observations still to be made, given the rich and varied way in which the New Testament writers quote and echo the Old Testament. You will discover more of this richness as you "read, mark, learn and inwardly digest"[15] the scriptures for yourself. And you will be participating in a discovery that Christians have been making throughout the history of the church.

I close with a stunning example from another era, showing how Christian interpreters have been sensitive to the relationship of the two testaments in the Christian Bible. Chartres Cathedral in France has the best collection of medieval stained glass windows. Practically the whole of biblical history is depicted in the glass and stones of that remarkable building. But I have a special fondness for the windows just below the great Rose in the south transept, because they offer a visual summation of the connection between the Old Testament prophets and the gospel writers. Malcolm Miller, the contemporary historian and tour guide of the cathedral, has offered this description of the windows:

> In the central lancet Mary, crowned with her child upon her arm, stands between four major prophets of the Old Testament, carrying astride their shoulders, the four New Testament evangelists, thus brilliantly demonstrating the concordance of the two testaments and the belief that Mary was the instrument whereby the Old

13. Stanley, *As it is Written*, 151 n.70.

14. Hays, *Echoes*, 39–41.

15. From the *Book of Common Prayer*, 184.

Testament prophecies were accomplished and the New brought through her son. On either side of her, from left to right, Jeremiah carries St. Luke, Isaiah carries St. Matthew, Ezekiel carries St. John and Daniel carries St. Mark. Like dwarfs on the shoulders of giants, the evangelists are smaller but see further, but only because the prophets have lifted them up. The Old Testament prepares for the New; the New is built upon the Old."[16]

FOR FURTHER EXPLORATION

Turn to 2 Cor 6:16–18. These verses contain a string of quotations from the scriptures of Israel. Look at these verses in several different versions to see how they are printed and formatted. Then choose one version that lists the Old Testament references at the bottom of the page, and note the differences in text-form (NRSV, NIV, CEB). Check your work against the very valuable table in Steve Moyise, *Paul and Scripture*.[17] What is the introductory formula, and are there words in the quoted material that emphasize the manner in which this catena of quotations is introduced? Then ask what was Paul's purpose in selecting these texts and bringing them together at this point in his argument in 2 Corinthians. After you have done these tasks, read the comments on these verses in a recent critical commentary, or best of all in the *Commentary on the New Testament Use of the Old Testament*. This exercise will be beneficial as you consider the material covered in the subsequent chapters of this book.

16. Miller, *Chartres*, 90

17. Moyise, *Paul and Scripture*, 92.

4

Application

IN THE PREVIOUS CHAPTER, we reviewed a number of Old Testament passages that were cited by multiple New Testament authors. This chapter will consider the variety of different elements in the New Testament preaching, teaching and apologetic to which a single Old Testament text might be applied. A single much-used passage might be employed by one writer as a testimony of the death and Resurrection of Jesus, by another to encourage Christian behavior, and by yet another to explain why Israel had not responded to the gospel. So, for example, Paul alludes to Isaiah 53 in Rom 4:25 to affirm that Jesus was "handed over to death for our trespasses, and was raised for our justification." We find the same application of Isaiah 53 to Christ's vicarious suffering in 1 Pet 2:24: "He himself bore our sins in his body on the cross." But the primary purpose for which Peter employs a number of phrases from Isaiah's Fourth Servant Song (Isaiah 53) in I Pet 2:21–25 is to encourage Christians to follow the example of Christ's patient trust in God under trial. Christ has left us "an example, so that you should follow in his steps." (2:21). In Matt 8:17, Isa 53:4 is quoted with Matthews's fulfillment formula and applied to Jesus' healing ministry: "This was to fulfill what had been spoken through the prophet Isaiah, 'He took our infirmities and bore our diseases.'" John also quotes from Isaiah 53, but he applies words from this chapter to the unwillingness of the religious leaders in Israel to believe in Jesus:

> 37 Although he had performed many signs in their
> presence, they did not believe in him,
> 38 This was to fulfill the word
> spoken by the prophet Isaiah:
> "Lord, who has believed our message,
> and to whom has the arm of the Lord been revealed?"
> (John 12:38)

The longest quotation from Isaiah 53 in the New Testament is found in Acts 8:32–33:

> Like a sheep that is led to the slaughter,
> And like a lamb silent before its shearers,
> So he does not open his mouth.
> In humiliation justice was denied him.
> Who can describe his generation?
> For his life was taken away from the earth.

Using these verses Luke simply records that Philip proclaimed to the Ethiopian Eunuch "the good news about Jesus." (Acts 8:35).

So we see that verses from a single passage in the Old Testament seemed to the earliest Christians to apply to a number of different elements in the Christian preaching, teaching and apologetic. To see for yourself how this works, take another passage from the scriptures of Israel that became very important for the early Christians: Psalm 22. First look at verse 1, which is quoted by Jesus in Mark 15:34 and Matt 27:46: "My God, My God, Why have you forsaken me?" Then note the way verse 19 is used in the passion narratives (Matt 27:35, Mark 15:24, Luke 23:34, John 19:24). Next observe how Heb 2:12 applies Psa 22:23. Then turn to Psalm 69. Here is another important scriptural testimony for the early Christians. Note how a portion of verse 10 is used in John 2:17, and another part of the verse is quoted by Paul in Rom 15:3. Then turn to Acts 1:20 to see a very different issue to which Psa 69:26 was applied by the early Christians.

In the previous chapter, I supplied a list of the numerous quotations, allusions and echoes of Psalm 110:1. If you look up these references in the New Testament, you will see that there are a variety of different issues for which the New Testament and other early Christian writers found this to be a key Old Testament text. Something of that variety was summarized by F.F. Bruce in lectures delivered at Fuller Theological Seminary in 1968, and later published under the title *This is That*.

> In Jesus the promise is confirmed,
> The covenant is renewed,
> The prophecies are fulfilled,
> The law is vindicated,
> Salvation is brought near,
> Sacred history has reached its climax,
> The perfect sacrifice has been accepted,
> The great priest over the household of God
> Has taken his seat at God's right hand,
> The Prophet like Moses has been raised up,
> The Son of David Reigns,
> The kingdom of God has been inaugurated,
> The Son of Man has received dominion
> From the Ancient of Days,
> The Servant of the Lord,
> Having been smitten to death
> For the peoples' transgressions
> And borne the sins of many,
> Has accomplished the divine purpose,
> Has seen light after the travail of his soul
> And is now exalted and extolled
> And made very high.[1]

MAPPING THE SHIFT OF APPLICATION

Of the many studies of the application of Old Testament texts in early Christianity, two in particular stand out. Barnabas Lindars' *New Testament Apologetic* (1961) and Donald Juel's *Messianic*

1. Bruce, *This is That*, 21.

Exegesis (1988) provide an excellent starting point for the careful study of this fascinating subject. Lindars studied the use of Old Testament testimonies primarily for their value as evidence of the earliest formulation of Christian doctrine. He asserted that

> The choice of quotation, the form of the text, and the method of interpretation, the context into which it is introduced, and comparisonof several citations of the same text , will all have to be taken into consideration, and may yield valuable evidence. [2]

Lindars' study asserted that when various applications of a given text are compared, it is sometimes possible to arrange them progressively. "In this way," he writes, "stages of interpretation can be discovered, corresponding to the developing thought and interest of the early church." [3] His primary example of a "shift of application" is the use of Isaiah 6:9–10:

> 9. And he said, "Go and say to this people:
> 'Hear and hear, but do not understand;
> see and see, but do not perceive.'
> 10 Make the heart of this people fat,
> and their ears heavy,
> and shut their eyes;
> lest they see with their eyes,
> and hear with their ears,
> and understand with their hearts,
> and turn and be healed.
> (RSV).

Lindars noted that in John 12:39–40, the quotation appears as a reason why the response to the mission of Jesus, and especially his signs, was so small. We find the same quotation in Acts 28:25–28 to explain the change of St. Paul's policy in turning from the Jews to the Gentiles.:

> 25 Paul made one further statement:
> "The Holy Spirit was right in saying to Your ancestors
> through the prophet Isaiah,

2. Lindars, *Apologetic*, 14.

3. Ibid. 17.

> 26 'Go to this people and say, You will indeed listen,
> but never Understand,
> And you will indeed look,
> but Never perceive.
> 27 For this people's heart has Grown dull
> And their ears are hard of Hearing
> And they will shut their eyes,
> So that they might not look With their eyes
> And listen with their ears
> And understand with their heart
> And turn – And I would heal them."
> 28 Let it be known to you then that this salvation of
> God has been sent to the Gentiles; they will listen
> (Acts 28:25–28).

In Mark 4:11–12, Isaiah's words are advanced as the reason why Jesus taught in parables. Lindars notes that "the Markan example has strayed into an entirely different field," and argues that "the shift of application shows the logical sequence in the development of thought." In this particular case, Lindars asserts, "the sequence of interpretation is the direct opposite of the presumed order in which the books themselves were written."[4]

Lindars' valuable study has been criticized by some scholars for presenting a particular progression of thought. His assertion that the Resurrection of Jesus is "the primary factor in the formation of Christian dogma"[5] came under review by Donald Juel in his important study, *Messianic Exegesis*. Juel began with the unmistakable observation that Jesus died *as a king*, "that Jesus was executed as a pretender to royalty, as King of the Jews."[6] This meant, according to Juel, that one of the key logical starting points for early Christian messianic exegesis was Psalm 89, understood in Jewish exegesis as a royal Psalm. Its application to Jesus as Messiah then suggested the relevance of other psalms to his career, especially to his humiliation and exaltation, namely Psalms 22, 31 and 69.

---

4. Ibid. 17.

5. *Ibid.* 29.

6. Juel, *Messianic Exegesis*, 25.

The problem with the approach of both Lindars and Juel is that they propose too tidy a development in early Christian thought and scripture exegesis. Different aspects of the gospel and its pre-figurement in the Old Testament impressed themselves on different early Christian leaders and communities in different locations, and close Christian networking led to a lively intellectual and spiritual growth in understanding. In one place the Resurrection caught the imagination, in another the Crucifixion or the Gentile mission. And these scholars' schemes, like those of many others, are not sufficiently attentive to the *prima facie* picture which we find in the New Testament, for example in Luke 24, that it was Jesus himself who was the "creative mind" who initiated the idea of suffering Messiah, and other aspects of the early Christian theology. Dodd's famous statement is worth quoting:

> To account for the beginning of this most original and fruitful process of rethinking the Old Testament we found need to postulate a creative mind. The Gospels offer us one. Are we compelled to reject the offer?[7]

Sometimes the application of Old Testament texts to elements of the Christian story will seem obvious and appropriate to the twenty-first century Western reader. At other times it will seem far-fetched, convoluted, or even fanciful. So, for example, Paul's use of Hab 2:4, "The righteous one shall live by faith" in Rom 1:17 seems to fit the argument, and as we observed in the previous chapter, Paul seems to have taken the context of Hab 1:1–2:4 into consideration. He is applying the text in a new situation while respecting the original context. But other texts seem to us to be more problematic. Take the example of the "Allegory of Hagar and Sarah" in Galatians 4:21–31. Paul argues :

> 24. Now this is an allegory(ἀλληγορούμενα) the women are the two covenants, the one woman, in fact, is Hagar, from Mount Sinai, bearing children for slavery. 25 Now Hagar is Mount Sinai in Arabia and corresponds to the present Jerusalem, for she is in slavery with her children. 26 But the other woman corresponds to the Jerusalem

7. Dodd, *Scriptures*, 110.

above; she is free, and she is our mother. 27 For it is written: "Rejoice, you childless one, you who bear no children, burst into Song and shout, you who endure no birth pangs; for the children of the desolate woman are more numerous than the children of the one who is married. (Isa 54:1).

Many contemporary readers will find Paul's "logic" difficult to follow. Some have argued that Paul's contemporaries had similar difficulties.[8] To our way of thinking Paul's argument here seems to be convoluted. He seems to us to be taking liberties and arguing on the basis of elements not found in the story of Genesis 21. For example, there is nothing in the story that corresponds to Ishmael persecuting Isaac, an assertion that Paul makes in verse 29. However, we need to be aware that, however strange his argument appears to us, he seems to be following exegetical practices that would have been common in his time and culture. It is important, therefore, in studying the way New Testament writers apply texts and stories from the Old Testament, that we understand the "rules of the game,"[9] the exegetical methods employed by Jewish exegetes of his day.

EXEGETICAL METHODS

What follows is a brief summary of the rules of interpretation common in Judaism in the Second Temple period. This list has been drawn from two recent valuable studies: E. Earle Ellis, *The Old Testament in Early Christianity*[10] and Craig A. Evans, *Jewish Exegesis.*[11] These are the so-called the "seven rules of Hillel the Elder." (died 10 CE). For each case I give a New Testament example of its use, and ask you to look up a second.

1. Qal wa –khomer, (literally, "light and heavy.") The rule states that what is true or applicable in a light or lesser instance

---

8. Stanley, *Arguing*, 130–135

9. Juel, *Messianic Exegesis*, 31.

10. Ellis, *Old Testament*, 89–90.

11. Evans, *DTIB*, 380–84.

must surely be true in a heavier or greater instance. A good example in the teaching of Jesus is Matt 6:30, "If God so clothed the grass of the field, which is alive today and tomorrow is thrown into the oven, will he not much more clothe you—you of little faith?" Now look at another example in 2 Cor 3:7–11. The crucial words are, "how much more. . .?"

2. *Gezerah shawah.* This rule literally means "an equivalent regulation." If a term or idea is found in two separate passages, they may explain or interpret one another. This inference from similar words may be observed in Rom 4:3–7. Here Paul explains the righteousness reckoned to Abraham (Gen 15:6) in terms of the forgiveness of Sins (Psa 32:1–2). The two are drawn together by a similar word, "reckoned" (ἐλογίσθη). Both Ellis and Evans point to Mark 2:23–28 as an example of Jesus' use of this rule of interpretation, drawing together the Son of Man from Dan 7:13–14 and 1 Sam 21:6. Can you find the similarity between the two passages that suggested the link?

3. *Binyan 'ab mikkkathub 'ekhad.* Constructing a general principle from one verse. In his argument with the Sadducees (Mark 12: 18–27 and parallels) Jesus argues from Exod 3:14–5, ("I am the God of your ancestors") that God has a continuing relationship with Abraham, Isaac and Jacob, and therefore these patriarchs, though dead are alive. On the basis of these verses Jesus argues for the resurrection. Look at Jas 5:16–17 and see how James establishes a general principle on the basis of one example from scripture.

4. *Binyan 'ab mishene ketubim.* Constructing a general principle from two verses. Paul argues from the command not to muzzle the ox (Deut 25:4) and to share sacrifices with the priests (Deut 18:1–8) that those who preach are entitled to support. (1 Cor 9:8–14). Now note how James employs two examples in Jas 2:22–26 to establish the general principle that faith is manifested by works.

5. *Kelal upherat upherat ukelal.* Literally, "General and particular and particular and general. When Jesus taught that the greatest commandment (the general)is to love the Lord with all one's heart (Deut 6:4–6) and to love one's neighbor as oneself (Lev 19:18) he sums up all the particular commandments. (Mark 12:28–34 and

parallels). Observe how Paul uses the same principle in Romans 13:8–10.

6. Kayotse bo mi-maqom 'akher. Inference from an analogous passage.

At Jesus' trial the High Priest asks, "Are you the Messiah, the Son of the Blessed One?" Jesus replied, "I am; and you will see the Son of Man seated at the right hand of the Power, and coming with the clouds of heaven." (Mark 14:62). Jesus draws together two Old Testament passages in a composite echo: Dan 7:13–14 and Psalm 110:1. Note how the author of the letter to the Hebrews (8:7–13) draws together two passages (Lev 26:9–12 and Jer 31:31–34) to argue for the necessity and the superiority of the new covenant.

7. Dabar halamed me 'inyano. A word of instruction from the context. Paul follows this rule in arguing that righteousness was reckoned to Abraham before he was circumcised (Gen 15:6) and this enables him to argue that Abraham is the father of both Jewish and gentile believers. (Rom 4:9–12). Note how Jesus uses the same rule of considering the context of Gen 1:27, 2:24, to argue against easy divorce, which some justified on the basis of Deut 24:1. (Matt 19:4–8).

TERMS AND TECHNIQUES

In order to understand Jewish exegesis of Scripture in New Testament times, it is important to be aware of the terminology used to describe their exegetical techniques. Among the most widely employed terms are the following:

Targums

The Targums were Aramaic translations of scripture, "free paraphrases, yet governed by certain laws." [12]This term refers to the attempt on the part of readers and interpreters to render the Hebrew scriptures into a language that people could understand. After the Babilonian exile in the sixth Century BCE most of the Jews spoke

---

12. McNamara, *Targum and Testament*, 119.

Aramaic rather than Hebrew, and there was a need to translate the scriptures as they were being read in public. The reader would give a line of Hebrew, and the translator (or *meturgeman*) would recite his translation. This practice can be traced back to Neh 8:8:

> So they read from the book, from the law of God, with interpretation. They gave the sense so that the people understood the reading.

Sometimes these targums attempted to be as literal as possible. But translation is always interpretation. And sometimes the targums are clearly interpretive. We saw one example of this in the Targum of Psa 68:18, where the targum reads "he gave gifts to people" instead of the Hebrew "He received gifts from people." And we saw that Paul follows the targumic rendering in Eph 4:8.[13] Craig Evans notes a number of instances where we can find targumic tradition in the New Testament. Perhaps the most striking instance is found in in Romans 10, where Paul creatively applies Deut 30:11–12 to Christ. Evans writes,

> At many points, Paul's allusive paraphrases and exegesis cohere with the Aramaic paraphrase, especially this is seen in *Targum Neofiti* (where instead of crossing the sea to fetch the law, we have Jonah descending into the depths to bring it up).[14]

Midrash

The word midrash is derived from the Hebrew word *darash*, which means to search or inquire after an answer. Among the many Old Testament examples we find Ezra the scribe, who "set his heart to search the law of the Lord." (Ezra 7:10). So the term comes to mean a running commentary that gives the sense of a biblical passage. The *Midrashim* in Rabbinic literature are running commentaries on the scriptures. Ellis asserts that as an interpretive activity midrash is oriented to scripture, adapting it to the present, for the purpose

---

13. See above, 8.

14. Evans, *DTIB*, 381.

of instructing or edifying the current reader or hearer. "It may take the form of either a simple clarification or a specific application of the texts."[15] We may note this procedure in operation in the Old Testament (The Old Testament Use of the Old Testament!). In Isa 19:19–22, where the prophet "transposes words and motif of Israel's redemption *from* Egypt (Exodus 1–12) to apply them to God's future redemption *of* Egypt.[16] It is fascinating to see the way the Exodus story is applied to the "new Exodus" in Isaiah 43, and the promise of return after seventy years of exile, prophesied in Jeremiah 25 is re-interpreted in Daniel 9. Look also at Paul's running commentary on the wilderness wanderings in 1 Cor 10: 1–13. This short entry only scratches the surface of a vast subject that illuminates much of the application of scripture in the New Testament.

Pesher

This term is used of a certain kind of midrashic technique used in the Dead Sea Scrolls. The *pesher* was the explanation of a mystery in the text. We find in the Habakkuk commentary scroll from Qumran a recurrent formula for the explaining and application of a text to the contemporary situation: "The pesher of this [Scripture] concerns the Teacher of Righteousness to whom God made known all the mysteries of the words of his servants the prophets" (1QpHab 7:4–5). [17] New Testament scholars have noted a similarity in assumptions and techniques in the New Testament in Matthew's formula quotations and in Peter's use of Joel in Acts 2.[18]

TYPOLOGY

Many scholars have found the term "typological interpretation" to be a leading method practiced by the earliest Christian writers, as they followed the practice of their Jewish contemporaries. Thus

15. Ellis, *Old Testament*, 92.

16. Ibid. 54.

17. Evans, *DTIB*, 383

18. See Chapter 1 above 4–6

"The Exodus provided a model or 'type' by which the prophets understood God's subsequent acts of redemption of Israel (Isa 40–66)"[19] Similarly, Adam prefigures Christ(Rom 5:14) Melchizedek Christ's high priesthood (Hebrews 7), the exodus and wilderness experience a prefigurement of the Christian pilgrimage (1 Cor 1:1–13). But recently it has been suggested that "typology" or "allegory" might not be the best terms to describe New Testament hermeneutic. These terms tend to suggest analogy with the allegorical exegesis associated with the Alexandrian school in the early church. Perhaps a better model is to be found in the homily patterns of the synagogue.[20] We will consider this proposal in the next chapter.

Haftarah: This term, which comes from the Hebrew p-t-r, "to conclude" refers to the sections from the prophets, that were linked to the Pentateuchal texts in the synagogue service, and were followed by an exposition. It is generally agreed that there are two examples of this practice in the New Testament: Jesus' sermon in the synagogue at Nazareth (Luke 4:16–19) and Paul's sermon in the synagogue at Antioch in Pisidia (Acts 13:13–41). These two passages offer evidence that this linking of the Haftarah and the reading of the Torah dates back to the second temple period.[21] Recent studies have suggested that attention to the Haftarot, and the Torah passages to which they were linked can shed light on a New Testament passages, especially where two or more Old Testament verses or stories are linked together. It is interesting to note that a further suggestion of Haftarah influence on the New Testament concerns the passage noted above, Gal 4:21–31. Here we see the combination of Gen 16:1 and Isa 54:1. A passage that seems difficult to us may be following accepted patterns and assumptions of Jewish exegesis.[22] But the subject of the combination of texts is so important that it deserves a chapter of its own, and will be the next topic to be considered.

---

19. Ellis, *Old Testament*, 105 note 113.

20. DiMattei, *As it is Wwitten*, 83.

21. Fishbane, *Haftarot*, xxiii.

22. DiMattei, "Biblical Narratives," 83 note 77.

FOR FURTHER EXPLORATION

In the first chapter, we saw that Paul quoted from the Song of Moses (Deuteronomy 32) three times in Romans. In each case he used a different text form.[23] Look up these three references:

> Rom 10:19 = Deut 32:21
> Rom 12:19 = Deut 32:35
> Rom 15:10 = Deut 32:43

What are the different issues in Christian faith and life to which these verses of the Song of Moses are being applied? Observe also that the three quotations from Deuteronomy 32 occur in Romans in the order of their occurrence in Deuteronomy. Do you think that Paul's logic in the latter half of Romans is being shaped by the Song of Moses?

23. See 6–7.

5

Combination

IN THE PREVIOUS CHAPTER we considered the term *Midrash*, a rabbinic term for the study and interpretation of scripture. One of the
features of midrash is the combination of two or more passages of
scripture, with a resultant interpretive effect. This phenomenon
can be found in many of the references to the Old Testament in
the New, and it deserves special study and attention. We will look
at two categories of midrash as it entails the combination of texts:
explicit midrash and implicit midrash.

EXPLICIT MIDRASH

We have already noticed several factors that led to the combination
of different texts from the Old Testament by the New Testament
authors. For example, in 1 Pet 2:6–8 the word "stone" was the catch-
word that drew together several texts (Isa 28:16, Psa 118:22 and Isa
8:14) under the interpretive principle of *Gezera Shewa*. [1] But the
variety of reasons for combining texts, and the diversity of methods

---

1. See p.21–22.

in doing so, which the New Testament writers employ is sometimes under-appreciated.

HOMILY PATTERNS

The pioneering work on the influence of Jewish exegetical patterns and techniques on the New testament writers was done by J.W. Doeve in 1954. He observed that some passages in the New Testament, especially Paul's speech in Acts 13:17–22, exhibited the features of a Jewish synagogue homily.[2] Doeve was followed by J.W. Bowker, who noted similar Jewish homiletic patterns in Acts 2,7 and 15.[3]

Based on these and other studies, E.Earle Ellis has shown that it is possible to detect behind a number of New Testament passages the traces of ancient Jewish homily patterns. Although the evidence we have for these patterns dates from a period later than the New Testament, it is striking to see how the New Testament bears witness to their existence in the synagogue preaching of the second temple period. Ellis remarked:

> While in the rabbinic collections these forms date from several centuries after the New Testament, they were hardly borrowed from the Christians. Also, similar patterns are present in the first-century Jewish writer, Philo. One may infer then, with some confidence, that their presence in the New Testament reflects a common, rather widespread Jewish usage.[4]

There were two types of homily patterns in Judaism, the *proem* and the '*yelammedenu rabbenu* midrashim, and both are reflected in the New Testament.

The rabbinic homily pattern generally took the following form:

---

2. Doeve, *Jewish Hermeneutic*, 172.
3. Bowker, *NTS* 14(1967–68), 96–111.
4. Ellis, *Old Testament*, 96.

—The (Pentateuchal) text for the day.

—A second text, the *proem* or "opening" for the discourse.

—Exposition

>Including supplementary quotations, parables and other Commentary with verbal links to the initial and final texts.

—A Final text

>Usually repeating or alluding to the text for the dayAnd sometimes adding a concluding application.

Ellis noted that in the New Testament this pattern is somewhat modified. For example, the New Testament writers do not begin with a Pentateuchal text, and the final text may not correspond or allude to the initial text. But these patterns in the New Testament show "an unmistakable resemblance to rabbinic midrash that cannot be co-incidental."[5] Let us look at the two types.

'yelammedenu rabbenu ("let our master teach us") Midrashim

This form begins with a question asked of a rabbinic teacher. In the gospels we find the form in discussions between Jesus and other Jewish theologians. Ellis gives as an example Matt 15:1–9, Jesus' discussion with the Pharisees and scribes concerning the tradition of the elders. Ellis shows that the passage conforms to the *yelammedenu rabbenu* pattern:

>15:1–4: Dialogue including an initial text: Deut 6:5; Lev 19:18.

>15:5–6 Exposition/application linked to the text and/or the dialogue
>>by the catchwords "honor" (4,6,8) "tradition" (3,6) "commandment/precepts (3,9).

>15:7–9 Concluding text (3,9).[6]

Now look up Matthew 19:3–9. Can you spot the Old Testament texts quoted in this dialogue and the catchwords that are incorporated in the discussion of these texts?

5. Ibid., 97.

6. Ellis, *Prophecy and Hermeneutic*, 158.

The Proem Homily Pattern

Whereas the *yelammedenu rabbenu* pattern is more common in the gospels, we find the *Proem* homily pattern in the Epistles. Such a *Proem* homily can be seen to underlie Paul's incorporation of scripture into his argument in Rom 9:6–29. Ellis notes the following correspondence:

> Rom 9:6–29
> 6 f. Theme and initial text: Gen 21:12
> 9 A second, supplemental text: Gen 18:10
> 10–28 Exposition containing additional citations (13, 15, 17, 25–28) and linked to the initial text by the catchwords "call" and "son" (12, 24ff., 27)
> 29 A final text(Isa 1:9) alluding to the initial text with the catchword "seed"[7]

Now turn to 1 Cor 1:18–31, and see whether you can find elements of the *proem* homily pattern in this section of the Letter. It is also to be observed that this shorter section in 1 Corinthians makes up a part of a larger *proem* homily pattern in 1 Cor 1:18–3:20.[8] Other passages that you might explore in the epistles, that Ellis claims exhibit elements of the rabbinic homily pattern, are Hebrews 10:5–39, Gal 4:21–5:1 and 2 Pet 3:5–13. Remember that not all New Testament passages will contain all the elements of the homily pattern, but a clear case can be made that these and other passages in the epistles contain some elements of it. Ellis noted that one striking example of the *proem* homily form in the gospels is found in Matt 21:33–46, and parallels, The parable of the wicked tenants. He outlined the pattern in this way:

> 33 Initial text (Isa 5:1f)
> 34–41 Exposition via a parable, verbally linked to the initial and /or
> final texts ("vineyard" 33, 39; "stone" 42, 44, cf 35:Isa 5:2; cf "build" "builders," 33,42).
> 42–44 Concluding texts (Psa 118:22f; Dan 2:34f.; 44f.)[9].

7. Ellis, *Prophecy and Hermeneutic*, 156.

8. Ibid., 157.

9. Ellis, *Old Testament*, 98.

A further interesting feature of this passage is the fact that the words "stone" (*eben*) and "son" (*ben*) may have sounded the same in Aramaic. It points to a Palestinian Aramaic link between the parable and the final texts. The Gospels represent Jesus as the "creative mind," and offer him as the one who made that link. Again I ask C.H. Dodd's question, "Are we compelled to reject the offer?"[10]

In this last passage considered, the parable of the wicked tenants, Jesus has taken a well-known parable from the Old Testament, and has re-interpreted it in terms of his own mission, rejection, death and resurrection. This use of the parable that applies it to a contemporary situation displays one of the fundamental features of midrash. It interprets Old Testament texts and stories so as to relate them to the present, and the near future. In the words of Ellis, midrashic homily patterns "consistently have an eschatological orientation."[11] This is the assumption behind Peter's exposition of Joel 2 in Acts 2, a speech that displays some features of homily patterns:

"This is what was spoken through the prophet Joel." (Acts 2:16).

With regard to Jewish homily patterns in the speeches in the Acts of the Apostles, it is interesting to note that the Old Testament quotations are "set entirely within Jewish contexts," and that the earliest Christians quoted scripture principally—if not exclusively within their mission to Jews. [12]

To discover for yourself how the New Testament writers comment on and contemporize Old Testament narratives, daringly appropriating them to their own situation, turn to 1 Cor 10:1–13. Note how Paul draws on the wilderness experience of Israel. Note also how he applies the story eschatologically, to the situation of the Corinthians (verses 6 and 11).

---

10. Dodd, *Scriptures*, 110. See 37.

11. Ellis, *Old Testament*, 97.

12. Longenecker, *Biblical Exegesis*, 96.

IMPLICIT MIDRASH

In addition to the many passages in the New Testament where the combination of Old Testament texts and stories, and their eschatological interpretation, indicate the employment of homily patterns current in the second temple period, there are a number of passages that are implicitly midrashic. Though the homily pattern is not present as such, the combination of texts appears to have left some trace of Jewish interpretive technique of this sort. In recent years there has been a growing awareness that midrash is not just a literary genre employed by Jewish writers but a broad-ranging interpretive activity.[13] Therefore, even though a homily pattern as such cannot be detected in passages which make reference to the Old Testament, midrashic assumptions and procedures may be in play. This is especially the case in composite quotations, allusions and echoes. These are scripture references where two or more Old Testament texts have been merged. Ellis noted that these type of citations often involve "either elaborate alterations of the Old Testament text or simple but significant changes of one or two words."[14]

Ellis noted several ways in which implicit midrash can be detected in New Testament writings. After noting that implicit midrash can be found in the Hebrew Old Testament, Biblical translations (LXX and Targums) and in the re-written Bible at Qumran (Genesis Apocryphon, Jubilees) He pointed to the implicit midrash in the nativity narratives in Matthew and Luke. Old Testament texts were brought together in the Song of Mary (*Magnificat*, Luke 1:46–55), the Song of Zacharias (*Benedictus*, Luke 1:68–79) and in the Song of Simeon (Nunc Dimitis, Luke 2:29–32). [15] It is a valuable exercise to take one of these canticles and try to discover how many Old Testament allusions and echoes you can find in the song. Take, for example, the shortest of the three, The *Nunc Dimitis*, or Song of Simeon, found in Luke 2:29–32.

J.A. Fitzmyer, in his commentary on Luke, has noted at least two Old Testament echoes in this brief song, and there may be

13. Vermes, *CHB* I,199–231.

14. Ellis, *Old Testament*, 95.

15. Ellis, *Old Testament*, 92–93.

more: For example, The 27th edition of Nestle/Aland also adds Psa 98:2. (The allusions from the Old Testament are in *italics*).

> 29 Now you may dismiss your servant, Lord, in
> peace, according to your promise,
> 30 for my eyes *have seen your salvation* Isa 40:5
> 31 made ready by you in the sight of all peoples,
> 32 *a light* to give revelation *to the Gentiles* and Isa 4:6
> glory to your people Israel.[16]

Now try to find the Old Testament allusions in one of the larger canticles, using whatever tools you have at hand: A cross-reference Bible or the margins of Nestle27. You may be surprised to discover how much these canticles allude to the Old Testament, combining verses from different places into a literary and theological composition.

COMPOSITE QUOTATIONS, ALLUSIONS AND ECHOES

One of the most fruitful areas for exploring implicit midrash in the New Testament is the composite, or merged quotations. These are quotations or allusions where a word or phrase from the Old Testament is merged with another. This can sometimes take the form of incorporation of a phrase into a longer passage. We have seen such an example in the chapter on text-form, where we saw that a phrase from Isaiah 58:6 is merged with the quotation from Isa 61:1–2 at Luke 4: 18–19.[17] The addition of the idea of release to the captives heightens the sense of jubilee and the end of exile. The additional line gives added theological depth to the programmatic preaching of Jesus. It may also indicate that the full homily that Jesus preached in the synagogue at Nazareth included exposition of the passages of Leviticus 25 (the year of Jubilee), Isa 61:1–2 (Good news to the poor and healing to the brokenhearted) Isaiah 58 (Release to the captives), and blessing and healing to the outsider(gentiles) as well

16. Fitzmyer, *Luke, I–IX*, 418.

17. See 2–3.

as to Israel (The woman of Zeraphath in Sidon and Naaman the Syrian). The midrashic pattern lies beneath the surface of Jesus' sermon at Nazareth.

Merged or composite citations can also be found in Paul's letters. We find this technique employed in the long catena of scripture text in Rom 3:10–18 and in his combination of several Old Testament passages in 2 Cor 6:16–18 in service of the assertion that "we are the temple of the living God." We can also see this phenomenon in Stephen's speech in Acts 7, where a number of texts are merged in a "running summary of the Patriarchal and Exodus story."[18] But some of the most fascinating instances of implicit midrash are to be found in the several composite quotations, allusions and echoes of the Old Testament in Mark.

MARK'S COMPOSITE ECHOES

An example of a composite quotation is found in Mark 1:2–3.[19] Here we see merged together phrases from Exod 23:20, Mal 3:1 and Isa 40:3. The merging together of these texts, together with the alteration of text in Mark 1:3 ("make his paths straight," applying to Jesus a text referring to "The Lord" in Isaiah) is clearly midrashic in character. This may also help to solve the curious problem of the introductory formula, where the attribution is to Isaiah, but the first words are from Malachi. Isaiah has supplied the key theological idea, "The way of the Lord," for what follows in Mark.

Similarly, in the voice at the baptism in Mark 1:11, "You are my son, the beloved; with you I am well pleased," we find a composite echo of three Old Testament texts: Psalm 2, Isaiah 42 and Genesis 22. As the texts are brought together they interpret one another.[20]

Now look at the story of Jesus "cleansing of the Temple," Mark 11:15–19. In 11:17 Jesus quotes scripture in support of his action:

> Is it not written,
> 'My house shall be called a house

18. Ellis, *Old Testament*, 95 note 66.

19. See 1.

20. See 14.

of prayer for all the nations?
But you have made it a den of robbers.'

This quotation from scripture combines two different Old Testament texts: Isa 56:7 and Jer 7:11. Commenting on this quotation, Nicholas Perrin has written recently,

> Jeremiah 7:11 and Isaiah 56:7 are not so much self-standing explanations but are the tip of a much larger homiletic iceberg, originating with Jesus and now hidden from the view of history.[21]

To discover for yourself the impact of Jesus' midrashic technique in drawing these two verses together, look up the two verses in their Old Testament contexts (Isaiah 56 and Jeremiah 7). These passages would have been known and studied by both Jesus and the religious leaders whom he challenges. As you read them over, can you feel combined impact that these passages would have had in the ears of their hearers as they were stitched together in Jesus' pronouncement from scripture?

Two other composite echoes in Mark are worth pondering. In Mark 14:62, in the context of Jesus' trial, the High Priest asks him, "Are you the Messiah, the Son of the Blessed one?"

> 62 Jesus said, "I am; and 'you will see the Son of Man seated at the right hand of the Power,' and 'coming with the clouds of heaven.'"

Here the imagery of Dan 7:14–15 is combined with that of Psa 110:1. It appears that Jesus' astounding claim to be both the Son of Man of Daniel 7 and the one Seated at the Right Hand of God in Psalm 110 was not misunderstood by those who heard it.

The claim may be yet more astounding, if we accept the old proposal, recently made by Daniel Boyarin, that when Jesus said "I am," (Eγώ εἰμι) he was not simply answering in the affirmative, but appropriating the divine name for himself.[22] If this is the case, it is interesting to note that in Mark 14:62 there are echoes from

---

21. Perrin, *Temple*, 84.

22. Boyarin, *The Jewish Gospels*, 138–39.

all three sections of the scriptures of Israel (Torah, prophets and writings).

The Son of Man of Daniel 7 is found in another composite echo in Mark. At Mark 10:45 it is combined with an allusion to the Servant of Isaiah 53:

> For the Son of Man came not to be served but to serve,
> And to give his life a ransom for many.

I believe that behind this summary statement of Jesus' mission we may imagine long sessions of teaching in which Jesus brought these two passages together after the manner of a homiletic midrash.

There are many other places throughout the New Testament where implicit midrash can be discerned through the combination of phrases from various passages of scripture. I was delighted to discover the three Old Testament allusions that Luke gives in the summary of Paul's speech to the Ephesian elders in Acts 20:28. Here, I believe, Paul echoes Psa 74:2, Gen 22:1, 16, and Isa 43:21.

> 28 to shepherd the church of God   —Psalm 74:2
> that he obtained   —Isa 43:21
> with the blood of his own Son.   —Gen 22:2[23]

FOR FURTHER EXPLORATION

To discover implicit midrash in the New Testament for yourself, look through any cross-reference Bible, and mark where a single New Testament verse alludes to more than one Old Testament passage. For a start, you might look at Matt 21:5. This is one of Matthew's "formula quotations" and it combines together two verses from different places in the Old Testament. Look the passages up in their Old Testament context and see where they lead. You may find this to be among the most exciting Bible studies you have ever performed.

---

23. Rodgers, *Text and Story*, 62–71.

6

History

INTRODUCTION

THE TERM "HISTORY" AS used in this study refers to the history of
biblical interpretation in Ancient Israel. Many of the Old Testament
texts found in the New Testament have also been quoted and interpreted by other Jewish groups and individuals in the centuries prior
to the rise of Christianity. Some of those texts were the subject of
intense speculation and specific application in Israel in the time of
Jesus. By studying the way in which these texts had been interpreted
in Judaism in the period, we can gain a deeper appreciation for the
ways in which the earliest Christians interpreted the same texts in
the light of Jesus. Indeed, a careful reflection on the Old Testament
and its use in the period demonstrates how the New Testament
authors fit nicely within Israel's tradition of re-appropriating the
scriptures in light of what God was doing in the present.

2 SAMUEL 7:14

We begin with an important Old Testament text, treated in the New Testament as a Messianic testimony. 2 Sa 7:11–14 records God's promise to David's heir through the prophet Nathan:

> 12 When your days are fulfilled
> and you lie down with your ancestors,
> I will raise up your offspring after you,
> who shall come forth from your body,
> and I will establish his kingdom.
> 13 He shall build a house for my name,
> and I will establish the throne of his kingdom forever.
> 14 I will be father to him,
> and he shall be a son to me.

Students of the New Testament know this "sure oath to David" (Psa 132:11) because it is applied to Jesus in Heb 1:5, and to Christians in 2 Cor 6:18. But those who study Messianic expectation in the period find a reference to this promise to David in the Psalms of Solomon, a work written in the middle of the first century BCE. The famous passage of Messianic expectation begins:

> See, O Lord, and raise up for them their
> king, the son of Dauid,
> at the time which you chose, O God, to
> rule over Israel your servant.[1]

The Psalm goes on to identify this descendant of David as "the anointed of the Lord" (Χριστὸς κυρίου). But when the Dead Sea Scrolls were discovered, they revealed how another group within Israel at the turn of the eras was interpreting 2 Sam 7:11–14. In a passage designated 4QFlorilegium we see how the Qumran sectaries, often identified as Essenes, combined this text with others in a collection of messianic testimonies:

> *The Lord declares to you that He will build you a House* (2 Sam. vii, 11c). *I will*

---

1. Psa Sol 17:21, NETS, 774.

> *raise up your seed after you* (2 Sam vii:12) *I will establish the throne of his kingdom [foe ever].* (2 Sam vii:13). *[I will be] his father and he shall be my son.* (2Sam. vii, 14). He is the Branch of David who shall arise with the Interpreter of the Law [to rule] in Zion [at the end] of time. As it is written, *I will raise up the tent of David that is fallen* (Amos ix, 11). That is to say, the fallen *tent of David* is he who shall arise to save Israel.[2]

Note that this collection of Messianic scripture texts found at Qumran combines 2 Sam 7:11–14 with Amos 9:11, a text also cited in the New Testament, in the speech of James at the Jerusalem council (Acts 15:15–18).

> 15 The prophets' words agree with this, as it is written,
> 16 *After this I will return,*
> *And I will rebuild David's fallen tent;*
> *I will rebuild what has been torn down.*
> *I will restore it*
> 17 *so that the rest of humanity will seek the Lord,*
> *even all the Gentiles who belong to me.*
> *The Lord says this, the one who does these things*
> 18 known from the earliest times. (CEB)

It seems that just prior to the time of Jesus these and other Mesianic scripture passages were very much in the air and were the subject of much hopeful speculation within Judaism. Indeed, the interpretation of these texts did not begin with the Second Temple period, but had already begun in the period when the later books of the Old Testament were being written. We find that 2 Sam 7:11–14 was applied to a new situation by both Isaiah 55 and Psa 132. The student of the Old Testament in the New Testament must begin with a study of the Old Testament in the Old.

ISAIAH 61:1–3

Another Old Testament text whose New Testament use is illuminated by setting it in the context of its use in Second Temple Judaism

---

2. Vermes, DSSE, 526.

is Isa 61:1–3. This is the text that Jesus read and commented on in his first sermon in the synagogue at Nazareth, where he had grown up. In the first chapter we studied the text form of this quotation as it appeared in Luke 4:18–19, and we compared it with the text form as found in the LXX of Isaiah 61:1–3.[3] Here we are interested in how other Jews of the period were interpreting this text. We noted in Luke's form of the text Jesus adds a line from Isa 58:6. This clearly heightens the sense of the Jubilee in this passage. A similar move and assumption is made in the Qumran text 11QMelchizidek. This fragmentary text reads: [the words in square brackets indicate where the text is fragmentary and had to be re-constructed]

> . . . And concerning which He said, *In [this] year of Jubilee [each of you shall return his property* (Lev. xxv, 13); *And this is the manner of release:] every creditor shall release that which he has lent [to his neighbor. He shall not exact from his neighbor or his brother], for God's release has been proclaimed*] (Deut. xv, 2). [And it shall be proclaimed at the end of days concerning the captives as [He said, *to pro-claim liberty to the captives* (Isa. lxi.i) Its interpretation is that He] will assign them to the Sons of Heaven and to the inheritance of Melchizedek; f[or He will cast] their [lot] amid the po[rtions of Melchize]dek who will return them there and will proclaim to them liberty, forgiving them [the wrong-doings] of all their iniquities. [4]

This fragmentary midrash continues with quotations from Psalm 132, Psalm 7, Isaiah 52 and Daniel 9, before returning to Isaiah 61:2–3:

> *To comfort [those who mourn: its interpretation]* to make them understand of T[ime] . . . In truth . . . will turn away from Belial . . . by the judgment[s] of God, As it is writ-ten concerning him, [*who saus to Zion*]; *your ELOHIM reigns. Zion Is.* . . , those who uphold the Covenant, who turn from walking [in] the way of The people. And *your ELOHIM* is [Melchizedek, who will save them from] the

3. See 2–3.

4. Vermes, *DSSE*, 532–33.

hand of Belial. As for that which He said, *Then you shall
send abroad the trump[et in] all the land* (Lev. xxv, 9). . . "

Fragmentary though this text from the Dead Sea scrolls is, it is
clear to see that 11Q Melchizedek, like Luke 4:18, interprets Isaiah
61 with the Jubilee of Leviticus 25. And just as the Qumran sectaries believed that these things were coming to pass in their own
time, and through their own community, so Jesus says in the synagogue at Nazareth, "Today this scripture has been fulfilled in your
hearing" (Luke 4:21). Comparative exegesis can help us to see a
similarity of assumptions and approach, but it can also give us a
keener understanding of the difference between the Qumran Sect
and Jesus and his followers. For whereas at Qumran Isaiah 61 was
interpreted to proclaim blessing to the insider and condemnation
to the outsider, Jesus' message offered blessing to the outsider. He
made this exegetical move by citing two examples of healing from
the ministries of Elijah and Elisha, in which outsiders were healed
reather than Israelites (The woman of Zerapath and Naaman the
Syrian).[5]

In the following exercise we will draw from what we have just
learned in the use of Isaiah 61 in both 11QMelchizidek and Luke
4, applying it to a similar situation in the history of interpretation.
First, compare the bolded sections in the passages below: 1) Luke
7:18–23 and 2) the Messianic Apocalypse, column 2 of 4Q521,
from the Qumran community:

1. Luke 7:18–23

> 18The disciples of John reported all these things to him.
> So John summoned two of his disciples 19and sent them
> to the Lord to ask, "Are you the one who is to come, or
> are we to wait for another?" 20When the men had come
> to him, they said, "John the Baptist has sent us to you to
> ask, 'Are you the one who is to come, or are we to wait for
> another?'" 21Jesus had just then cured many people of
> diseases, plagues, and evil spirits, and had given sight to
> many who were blind. *22And he answered them, "Go and
> tell John what you have seen and heard: the blind receive*

5. Sanders, "From Isaiah 61 to Luke 4," 75–106. Rodgers, *Text and Story*,
93–100.

> *their sight, the lame walk, the lepers are cleansed, the deaf*
> *hear, the dead are raised, the poor have good news brought*
> *to them.* 23And blessed is anyone who takes no offense
> at me."

2. 4Q521

> [. . . for the heav]ens and the earth will listen to his
> Messiah, [and all] that is in them will not turn away
> from the commandments of the holy ones. Strengthen
> yourselves, you who are seeking the Lord, in his service!
> Will you not in this encounter the Lord, all those who
> hope in their heart? For the Lord will consider the pious
> and call the righteous by name, and his spirit will hover
> upon the poor, and he will renew the faithful with his
> strength. For he will honor the pious upon the throne
> of an eternal kingdom, *freeing prisoners, giving sight to*
> *the blind,* straightening out the twis[ted.] And for[e]ver
> shall I cling to [those who] hope, and in his mercy [. . .]
> and the fru[it of . . .] not be delayed. And the Lord will
> perform marvellous acts such as have not existed, just
> as he sa[id, for] he will *heal the badly wounded and will*
> *make the dead live; he will proclaim good news to the poor*
> and [. . .] he will lead the [. . .] *and enrich the hungry.*
> [. . .] and all [. . .][6]

In the following chart, attempt a list of similarities between the two
texts as influenced by the Isaianic echoes found in both passages
(Isa 29:18–19; 35:5–6; 42:18; 43:8; and 61:1).

Luke 7	4Q521

<hr />

6. 4Q521 frgs. 2 ii 1–14 in Florentino Garcìa Martìnez, *The Dead Sea*
*Scrolls : Study Edition.*1045.

Joel B. Green has aptly referred to this symphony of echoes as a "festival of salvation."[7] It is no accident that the material here harks back to Jesus' inaugural proclamation in Nazareth, where he first proclaimed his anointed mission. However, not all the material here harks back to that inaugural address, nor do all of the Messianic expectations as transmitted in the text from Qumran appear in Luke. Can you observe one feature in 4Q521 that is strikingly absent in Luke's account? If you need a hint, consider "where" John the Baptist is situated when he sends his disciples to Jesus. Could it be that these contemporary Messianic expectations, as evidenced in 4Q521, were also feeding John's hopes? If so, perhaps Jesus is responding to the very source of John's doubts, drawing a circle around it with his silence, if you will. Have you discovered it?

(See the end of this chapter for a completed chart and check your work against it)

ISAIAH 28:16

Another Old Testament text used by both New Testament writers and the Qumran community is Isa 28:16. "Therefore thus says the Lord God, See I am laying in Zion a foundation stone, a tested stone, a precious cornerstone, a sure foundation: one who trusts will not panic." This verse is found in both 1 Peter (1 Pet 2:6) and Romans (Rom 9:33). It is also found in the Dead Sea scrolls, and is used by the writer of the Manual of Discipline to show how the community, when living in obedience to the teachings of the Teacher of Righteousness was fulfilling this ancient Isaianic promise:

> When these are in Israel, the Council of the Community shall be established in truth. It shall be an Everlasting Plantation, a House of Holiness for Israel, an assembly of Supreme Holiness for Aaron. They shall be witness to the truth at the judgment, and shall be the elect of Good-will who shall atone for the land and pay to the wicked their reward. It shall be that tried wall, that *precious*

7. Green, *Luke*, 279.

> *Corner-stone*, whose foundations shall neither rock nor
> sway in their place. (Isa. xxviii, 16)[8]

But the "stone laid in Zion" of Isa 28:16 appears to have had
a rich history of interpretation before it is cited by Qumran or the
New Testament. We note that the Septuagint translator of this verse
makes an addition to the Hebrew form that paves the way for applying this verse to the Messiah and the messianic community. Note
the words in italics:

> Therefore thus says the Lord,
> See, I will lay for the foundations of Sion
> a precious, choice stone
> a highly valued cornerstone for its
> foundations,
> and the one who believes *in him* (ἐπ' αὐτῷ) will not
> be put to shame.[9]

The addition of *in him* (or *in it*) in the LXX has already begun
an interpretive process that will issue in the full eschatological and
messianic interpretations in the New Testament era.

THEOLOGICAL MOTIVATION
BEHIND TEXTUAL CHANGE

Sometimes changes to a text of the scriptures of Israel can signal
both literary and theological concerns. Take, for example the addition of the term "light" in the Isaiah scrolls a, b, and d and in the
LXX of Isa 53:11, a term lacking an equivalent in Masoretic text.
"*Out of the suffering of his soul he will see light.*"[10]

Emanuel Tov has drawn attention to theologically motivated
changes in the text of the Hebrew Bible in a number of passages. His
example of the changes in Deuteronomy 32, the Song of Moses, are
instructive and important for students of the Old Testament in the
New, because this passage plays a prominent role in the formation

8. 1Qs VIII 5–8; Vermes, *DSSE*, 109.

9. NETS 844.

10. Abegg, Flint and Ulrich, *The Dead Sea Scrolls Bible*, 360.

of New Testament theology (Paul quotes from this chapter three times in Romans[11]). Tov notes the following differences between the MT and the LXX and Qumran:

(The Text presented here is that of the MT. The LXX colons additional to the MT are printed in bold between + signs, while differences between the two are italicized. Agreements between the LXX and the Qumran scroll, 4Q Deutq are indicated)

Tov gives this presentation of Deut 32:43:

43 (a) Gladden/acclaim, O nations, his people MT / *Be glad, O skies with him.* LXX = 4Q Deutq
    (b) **+ And let all the sons of God do obeisance to him +** = 4Q Deutq
    (c) **+ Be glad, O nations, with His people +**
    (d) **+ And let all the angels of God prevail for Him. +**
    (e) For he'll avenge the blood of his servants MT / *sons* LXX
    (f) wreak revenge on His foes MT / *and take revenge and repay the enemies with a sentence* LXX
    (g) **+ and he will repay those who hate + =** 4Q Deutq
    (h) and the Lord will cleanse the land of his people. MT

Tov commented:

> It seems that the MT shortened the long version of the LXX and the Qumran scroll. One detail supporting this assumption is the incomplete poetic structure of 43 in the MT, rendering the additional colons necessary.[12]

He further comments that the shortening of LXX and Qumran by MT was likely due to the concern that God should wreak vengeance on Israel's enemies, rather than that they should join Israel in praising God. A further concern of the MT change is that the phrase "sons of God" was considered "an unwelcome polytheistic depiction of the world of the divine." [13]

---

11. See 7.
12. Tov, "The Septuagint as a Source," 41.
13. Tov, "The Septuagint as a Source," 43.

We have already noted that Paul quotes from Deuteronomy 32 three times in Romans. [14] Look back at Paul's citations of this important passage from the Old Testament, and see how they may have light shed on them in view of this developing interpretive tradition.

RETELLING THE EXODUS

Biblical interpretation in Israel can shed light on New Testament interpretation of the Old Testament, not only in these significant changes, whether large or small, noted above, but also in the treatment of larger passages and stories in the literature of the Second Temple period. We have noted Luke's addition of the reference to Jesus' "Exodus" in his account of the transfiguration (Luke 9:31). We also note that Paul drew on and contemporized the story of the Exodus and the wilderness experience of Israel in 1 Cori 10:1–13, and Peter's exhortation in 1 Pet 1:13–20 is certainly shaped by the exodus story. Moreover, recent studies have shown how the Exodus theme undergirds the formation of the Gospel of Mark and The Acts of the Apostles. [15] But it is clear that the Exodus story had been much studied, told and retold in ancient Israel. Even in the canonical Old Testament we find the re-telling of the Exodus story, with application to a new situation in which the people of God find themselves. Look at Psalm 78 and Isaiah 43, and see if you can detect how the Exodus story is being told and applied to Israel at different points in her history. This constant re-telling of the Exodus story is understandable in light of the annual celebration of Passover and the recitation of the Passover *Haggadah*.

Peter Enns, in his book *Exodus Retold*, studies how the story of the Exodus is re-told in the Wisdom of Solomon 10:15–21 and 19:1–9. Enns has shown how this document, written around the turn of the eras makes use of older traditions of the Exodus story

---

14. See 7.

15. Watts, *Isaiah's New Exodus in Mark*, Pao, *Acts and the Isaianic New Exodus*.

and anticipates further developments in Jewish literature. Enns writes,

> At the time that the Wisdom of Solomon was written (Between 100 BC and 50 AD) there already existed an extensive and well-developed set of exegetical traditions concerning the Pentateuch in particular.[16]

Thus, he observes, we need to study the Exodus story in the whole range of Jewish literature in the period and beyond. This includes both the canonical scriptures, the Apocrypha and Pseudepigrapa , Philo and Josepheus, Qumran and the Rabbinic literature. It also includes the New Testament use of the Exodus story as part of the developing interpretive tradition. If this seems a daunting task, the student should persevere, since the rewards are great, and there is still so much to discover.

Already in the Hebrew Bible, we find various re-tellings and applications of the exodus story. The interpretative traditions of this story continued to grow and develop in Judaism. A fascinating example of this continued interpretive embellishment of the Exodus can be found in the Palestinian Targum on the Pentateuch. The forms in which we have this targumic paraphrase of Exodus 12 (the Passover story) comes from a later date than the New Testament. But a number of the elements of this developed tradition can be traced back to the second temple period.

THE EXODUS AND THE SACRIFICE OF ISAAC

Exodus 12:42 reflects on the significance of the Passover:

> 42. That was for the Lord's night of vigil, to bring them out of the land of Egypt. The same night is a vigil to be kept for the Lord by all the Israelites throughout their generations.

This brief reflection on the importance of celebrating the Passover has been expanded in the Palestinian Targum on Exodus into

16. Enns, *Exodus Retold*, 11–12.

the elaborate and beautiful "Poem of the Four Nights." The "Four Nights" of the poem are:

> The night of creation
> The night of Abraham and Isaac
> The night of the Passover
> The night of the Messiah.

The portion of the poem that has generated considerable discussion is the second section: the night of Abraham and Isaac. In the Palestinian Targum it reads:

> Was not our father Isaac a son of thirty and seven years at the time he was Offered upon the altar? The heavens were then bowed down and brought low, And Isaac saw their realities and his eyes were blinded at the sight, and he called it the Second night.[17]

Geza Vermes noted a number of distinctive features in this developed tradition of the Passover. Chief among them is the link between the Passover and the Sacrifice of Isaac. (Exodus 12 and Genesis 22). This link had already been made in the second century BCE in the *Book of Jubilees*, which set the Sacrifice of Isaac on the 14th Nisan (the time when the Passover was celebrated). A number of other elements of the developed interpretive tradition on Genesis 22 can be traced to the second temple period. These may be found in the writings of Jubilees, Josephus, IV Maccabees, and LAB (Pseudo-Philo). These particular elements are: Isaac's adult age, Isaac informed, Isaac's consent, the merit of Isaac, The temple mount (Mount Moriah) as the place of sacrifice, and the idea of the blood or ashes of Isaac.[18] Vermes has produced a useful table of illustrating the developed tradition.[19] He concludes that it is possible to trace "a pre-Christian skeleton of the targumic-midrashic representation of the sacrifice of Isaac."[20]

---

17. Etheridge, *The Targums*, 480.

18. Vermes, *Scripture and Tradition*, 193–227.

19. Vermes, *Jewish Context*, 113.

20. Ibid. 113.

Some scholars questioned Vermes' reconstruction of a developed Isaac tradition in the second temple period. Davies and Chilton especially posited that it was a product of rabbinic Judaism in the era after the rise of Christianity, and perhaps a response to it.[21] Others found it compelling and valuable for their own work.[22] Then, in 1995, a fragmentary document was published from among the Dead Sea Scrolls that gave further evidence of a developed *Akedah* (binding of Isaac) tradition in the second temple period.[23] Here is one place, among many, where new discoveries, especially among the Dead Sea Scrolls, have helped to fill in the gaps in tracing the history of the interpretation of the Old Testament in the era that saw the rise of Christianity.

THE END OF EXILE

It is important for the student of the Old Testament in the New to realize that the Christian interpreters of the Scriptures of Israel are participating in developed and still developing traditions of interpretation. This fact came home to me through a study of Daniel 9, and the prayer for the end of the exile. In Daniel 9 the prophet perceives, through reading Jeremiah 25, that it is time for the exile to be over. Yet he recognizes that Isreal is still in Exile. It is revealed to him that the 70 years predicted by Jeremiah are actually 70 weeks of years. This is an interpretive application of the prophecy of Jeremiah to a new situation. But the prophecy had already been re-interpreted in 2 Chronicles 36:18–21. Here the Chronicler re-interprets the oracle of Jeremiah by combining it with the provision for the years when Israel did not observe the Jubilee in Lev 26:34–5. Here is 2 Chronicles 36:18–21, with the words from Lev 26:34–5 in *italics*:

> And they[the Chaldeans] burnt the house of God, and broke down the walls of Jerusalem. . .to fulfil the word of YHWH by the mouth of Jeremiah, *until the land has*

21. Davies and Chilton, "The Akedah," 514–546.

22. Levenson, *Death and Resurrection*, 173–199.

23. 4Q225. Vermes, DSSE, 451.

> *made up for its sabbaths; for all the time that it lay desolate*
> *it rested* to fulfil 70 years.[24]

This early re-interpretation of the Jeremiah 25 prophecy continues to develop in Israel in the second temple period, and since the sense of ongoing exile is an important backcloth to the teaching of Jesus and early Christianity, it is vital to set the New Testament in the context of this developing interpretive history.[25]

FOR FURTHER EXPLORATION

This chapter has only scratched the surface of a vast and fruitful area of study and research. We have begun to see some of the fruit that comes from comparing the apostolic exegesis of the Old Testament with the history of exegesis that was already developing in the Old Testament and post-biblical Judaism. For some coming to these issues for the first time, grasping the amount of material that comes from this period may seem like a daunting task. My hope is that the examples presented in this chapter have stimulated your interest to consider how you might become a participant in this rich conversation. Perhaps no resource will be more valuable to you as you begin this study than Beale and Carson, *Commentary on the New Testament Use of the Old Testament*.

The wealth of material collected in this volume will provide an excellent starting point for your own exploration.

For others coming to this study for the first time, it may be unsettling to study the changes made to the canonical text of scripture. But the more one appreciates the disciplined freedom with which the New Testament writers interpret the Old Testament in the light of Jesus the Messiah, the more one begins to understand the dual nature of the scripture as both human writing and Holy Scripture. If we allow the actual nature of the documents of scripture to lead us in the direction of their own, their historical and canonical context, we can only grow in both knowledge and reverence.

24. Fishbane, *Biblical Interpretation*, 481.
25. Wright, *Jesus and the Victory of God*, 234–35.

As an exercise in the history of interpretation of an Old Testament text in the New Testament and early Christianity I suggest a study of Isa 52:5. This text is quoted in Rom 2:24 in its LXX form. "For the name of God is blasphemed among the Gentiles through you, as it is written." (KJV). Note the differences from the Hebrew (MT) as printed in the NRSV. (form) Note also the curious way the introductory formula comes after the quotation, rather than in the usual place in Paul, before the cited text (reflected in the KJV). (introduction). Observe that Paul's use of the text in Romans 2, though sometimes considered random and arbitrary, serves Paul's purpose and has been carefully selected.(selection). Consider Paul's application of the text. Paul's point throughout the paragraph is, as N.T. Wright notes, "that Israel as a whole is not living up to what YHWH would desire, and that Israel's continued subservience to the pagan nations, which had begun with the Babylonian captivity, was a sign that the great promised redemption had not yet arrived. In other words, Israel's 'exile' was still continuing. . ."[26] (application). Look at Romans 2 and ask whether Paul cites any other Old Testament texts in the near context (combination). Now look at Ezek 36:20. This passage somewhat ante-dates Isa 52:5, so the latter is a first stage in the history of the long application of this verse in the history of Israel and the church.[27] It seems that lots of people were thinking about the name of God, blasphemed among the gentiles in Judaism and early Christianity (history). Where do you think that Paul fits in to the developing history of the interpretation of Isa 52:5?

PROPOSED ANSWERS TO THE CHART COMPARING LUKE 7 AND 4Q521

If we are right in our assumption that John's expectations were fed by those similar to the list in 4Q521, he must have been wondering, "if you are the Messiah, why am I still in prison?" Strikingly absent in Jesus' reply is any reference to "freeing prisoners"! The message must have been clear, though stated in rich and nuanced

26. Wright, *Romans*, 447.

27. Lindars, *New Testament Apologetic*, 22–24.

Jewish exegetical form: "though jailbreak is not on my immediate political platform, I am certainly the One who has Come!" This interpretation also helps elucidate the strange closing beatitude of this section: "And blessed is anyone who takes no offense at me." Jesus, with yet another possible Isaianic echo (here from Isa 8:14), appeals for John and all others not to take offense at/be snared by (μὴ σκανδαλισθῇ ἐν ἐμοί.) him.

Possible answers to chart:

Luke 7	4Q521
Curing many of diseases	Healing the wounded
Blind being "benefacted" sight	Making the blind see
Dead are raised up	Make the dead live
Poor have good news preached	Poor have good news preached

7

Story

In the 1990's I experienced a major shift in my understanding of the New Testament, and in particular of the New Testament use of the Old Testament. In short I discovered that Jesus, Paul and the other New Testament writers were not so much declaring timeless truths and moral precepts as telling a story: the story of God and his people. This change in my thinking came about primarily through reading the works of two influential biblical scholars, N.T. Wright and Kenneth Bailey.

N.T. WRIGHT

Wright's influential book, *The New Testament and the People of God*, was fundamental to this shift in my thinking. His book reminded me that "telling stories was . . . one of Jesus' most characteristic modes of teaching."[1] Thus he introduced me in a fresh way to Jesus as a narrative theologian. With regard to St. Paul, Wright asserted that

1. Wright, *New Testament*, 77.

Paul is telling, again and again, the whole story of God, Israel and the world as now compressed into the story of Jesus. So, too, his repeated use of the Old Testament is designed not as mere proof-texting, but in part at least, to suggest new ways of reading well-known stories, and to suggest that they find a more natural climax in the Jesus story than elsewhere.[2]

What was clear to me from reviewing Wright's large and ongoing project entitled *Christian Origins and the Question of God* is that the use of Old Testament by Jesus and the writers of the New Testament was the retelling of "*the essentially Jewish story now redrawn around Jesus.*"[3] The major contours of the story Jesus retold are creation and covenant, Exodus and exile, kingship and Messiah. The Old Testament stories, whether in Genesis or Kings or Psalms or Isaiah, are all expressive of this narrative world which was now being re-drawn around Jesus, the one who is the climax of that story, and through whom the kingdom of God is finally and decisively breaking in.

Wright's insistence on seeing Jesus in the context of the Jewish story opened up for me a new way of reading the parables of Jesus. Thus the Parable of the Wicked Tenants (Matt 21:33–46, Mark 12:1–12, Luke 20:9–19, Gospel of Thomas 65) is a clear echo of the Parable of the vineyard of Isaiah 5, which Jesus is re-telling as the story of Israel with himself at the center. This is achieved by the combination of the parable with Psa 118:22:

The stone that the builders rejected has become the cornerstone;
This is the Lord's doing, and it is amazing in our eyes.
(Mk 12:11).

This combination of Old Testament texts in Jesus' re-telling of the parable is further enhanced by an allusion to Gen 22:2, 16. Here the "son" that is sent is described as the "beloved" or "only" son (υἱὸν ἀγαπητόν). In the previous chapter we noted the importance of this particular Old Testament story of the Sacrifice of Isaac for

2. Ibid., 79.
3. Ibid., 79.

Jews of the second temple period. The combination of these three Old Testament texts in no small measure drives Jesus' re-telling of the story of Israel with himself, the "rejected stone/son" at the center. It is also interesting to note that the three texts found in combination here are from the three divisions of the TaNaK or Hebrew Old Testament: the Law, the Prophets and the Writings.

THE SOWER AND OTHER PARABLES

Wright's storied analysis of the Parable of the Wicked Tenants seemed clear to me, but at first other proposals about the parables of Jesus seemed far-fetched. In particular his reading of the Parable of the Sower (Mark 4:1–20, Matt 13:1–23, Luke 8:4–18, Gospel of Thomas 9) led me to wonder whether he was over-reading the text. Wright commented on this Parable:

> The parable tells the story of Israel, particularly the re-
> turn from exile, with a paradoxical conclusion, and it
> tells the story of Jesus' ministry as the fulfillment of that
> larger story, with a paradoxical outcome.[4]

I had always read the parable as indicating how different people respond to the word of God. Wright invited readers to see a broader, corporate, even political dimension to the story. The parable was about God, "sowing his people again in their own land."[5] My first reaction was that this was far-fetched. I also felt that his claim that certain chapters of Daniel, particularly chapters 2 and 7, were also being echoed in this parable was intriguing but not entirely convincing. But what drew me to his proposal was the assertion of a background for this chapter in Isaiah 55, and his discussion of Isaiah 6:9–10. Wright observed that above all

> The book of Isaiah used the image of sowing and reap-
> ing as a controlling metaphor of the great work of new
> creation that God would accomplish after the exile. "The
> Grass withers and the flower fades, but the word of our

4. Wright, *Jesus and the Victory of God*, 230.
5. Wright, *Challenge*, 40.

> God will stand forever. As the rain and the snow water the earth, so shall my word be. It shall not return to me empty but it will accomplish my purpose," New plants, new shrubs will spring up before you as you return from exile.[6]

Wright's treatment of the quotation from Isaiah 6 in Mark 4:10–12 and parallels was equally compelling. They must "look and look and never see. . ." Just after the portion quoted from Isa 6:9–10 the prophet asks, "How long, O Lord?"

And the long oracle of judgment ends with verse 13:

> Even if a tenth part remain in it, it will be burned again.
> Like a terebinth or an oak whose stump remains standing when it is felled.
> The holy seed is its stump.

Wright asserted that the parable of the sower evokes Isaiah 6 "not accidentally, or obliquely, but by way of *telling the story of Israel as the story of rejected prophets, consequent judgment, and renewal on the other side of judgment.*"[7] I was won over by this Old Testament sensitive way of reading the text of Mark 4, drawn in the direction that the quotations and allusions led me. My eyes were opened to the way in which the parable of the sower fit into the larger narrative of God and his people.

Another of Wright's proposed interpretations of parables cemented for me this narrative way of thinking with regard to the teaching of Jesus. This is the parable of the growing seed. (Mark 4:26–29)

> 26. He also said, "The Kingdom of God is as if someone would scatter seed on the ground 27 and would sleep and rise night and day, and the seed would sprout and grow, he does not know how. 28 The earth produces of itself first the stalk, then the head, then the full grain in the head. 29 But when the grain is ripe, at once he goes in with his sickle, because the harvest has come.

6. Wright, *Challenge*, 40, quoting Isa 40:8, 55:10–11, 13.

7. Wright, *Jesus and the Victory of God*, 236, italics his.

I once heard Wright comment that if Jesus had simply been commenting on the farming practices of the day nobody would have crucified him! He is rather speaking here in parables of coming Judgment. But how do we know this? Wright's clues for understanding the parable are found in the allusions to the Old Testament, just beneath the surface, that would not be missed by first century Jews. The first expression drawn from the Old Testament is the phrase "When the grain is ripe, at once he goes in with the sickle, because the harvest has come." This is an allusion to Joel 3:13, found near the end of a book that is all about the "coming day of the Lord." This coming day of judgment "won't look like what they were expecting," notes Wright. "God is not simply vindicating Israel and condemning those outside. When Judgment comes, it will look rather different. But come it will."[8]

The second allusion is found in the seemingly mundane description of the farmer who "would sleep and rise, night and day, and the seed would sprout and grow, he does not know how." (Mark 4:27). This is a clear reference to the Creation story in Genesis 1 with its repeated "And there was evening and there was morning,. . ." (Gen 1:5). Wright also noted the allusion to Gen 8:22, where God resolves not to destroy the earth after the flood:

> 22 As long as the earth endures,
> seedtime and harvest, cold and heat,
> summer and winter, day and night
> shall not cease.

Other commentators on Mark had noticed these allusions to the scriptures of Israel in this brief parable. But it was Wright who made the clear connection to the larger narrative of God and his people presented in scripture. I could no longer read parables as isolated teachings of Jesus, designed to impart timeless truth and moral lessons. They were all expressive of the Story.

8. Wright, *Mark for Everyone*, 48.

KENNETH BAILEY

Kenneth E. Bailey has spent his life as a student of the New Testament in its Middle Eastern cultural setting. I heard him lecture on the parable of Jesus in 1997 and subsequently read his book *Finding the Lost, Cultural Keys to Luke 15*. In this book Bailey tells of his life-long love affair with Luke 15 (the chapter containing the parables of the Lost Sheep, the Lost Coin, and the Prodigal Son). Bailey narrated in the book his discovery of a great key for understanding these parables, especially the last one.

> Having for decades made Luke 15 the centerpiece of my understanding of Jesus and the New Testament, and having tried to read everything of note—East and West— that had been written in the past and present on this chapter, I thought I had done my homework on all the important aspects of the three parables that the chapter contains.

Bailey then relates how he stumbled on to a new way of understanding the chapter that he likened to a chest full of gold. "This was the discovery of the fact that Luke 15 can be seen as an expansion of Psalm 23."[9] He outlined in detail 13 themes that Luke 15 shares with Psalm 23. His final chapter is entitled "Luke 15 and Psalm 23, a Vision Expanded."[10] Subsequently, Bailey has produced a book entitled *Jacob and the Prodigal*. Careful observation led him to propose 51 points of comparison and contrast between Genesis 27–35 (The story of Jacob) and Luke 15:11–32 (The Prodigal Son).[11] Bailey's work on Luke 15 cemented what I had already discovered through my reading of N.T. Wright. The New Testament writers, and Jesus behind them, did not merely quote or allude to Old Testament stories as they were convenient for the arguments they were making. Rather, they lived in the *story* of God and his people, and this story was the source of all life and thought to all Jews in the second temple period.

---

9. Bailey, *Finding the Lost*, 10–11.

10. Ibid. 194–212.

11. Bailey, *Jacob and the Prodigal*, 216–218.

I would go so far as to assert that for me two of the most important books in New Testament studies in the last twenty years are N.T. Wright's *The New Testament and the People of God* and Kenneth Bailey's *Finding the Lost*.

FINDING THE STORY

Just as I discovered the broader narrative dimension, the Story of God and his people, behind and beneath the surface of the parables of Jesus through the reading of Wright and Bailey, so I invite you, at the end of this chapter to do your own discovery and exploration. Look at other parables of Jesus and ask yourself two questions. 1) Are there any Quotations, allusions or echoes of the Old Testament in this parable? 2) How do these Old Testament references relate to the *story* of God and his people, the story of Creation and Covenant, of Exodus and Exile, of Kingship and Messiah? You might start with the parable of the Mustard Seed (Mark 4:30–32).

> 30 He continued, "What's a good image for God's kingdom? What parable can I use to explain it? 31 Consider a mustard seed. When scattered on the ground, it's the smallest of all the seeds on the earth; 31 but when it's planted, it grows and becomes the largest of all vegetable plants. It produces such large branches that the birds of the sky are able to nest in its shade." (CEB)

Ask yourself, are there any quotations, allusions of echoes of the Old Testament in this parable? To hunt these down, look at the notes in any good reference Bible, or in the margins of the Nestle27 Greek New Testament. I found two Old Testament references in my New Scofield Reference Bible, which I have owned for years. They were sitting there waiting to be discovered. Look up the passages referred to, and ask how they relate to the larger story of God and his people. When you have got this far, turn to the *Commentary on the New Testament Use of the Old Testament.* Here you will find several pages of discussion on this parable and the Old Testament echoes in it. Rikk E. Watts, who writes the section on Mark gives some very helpful remarks on the broader narrative features of this parable brought to light by the Old Testament allusions and echoes.[12]

N.T. Wright noted that "the narrative analysis of parables is yet in its infancy."[13] There is still much work to be done, and still many unnoticed ways in which the New Testament writers, in their use of the Old Testament, point to the grand narrative of God and his people.

FOR FURTHER EXPLORATION

Many commentators have observed that the story of Jesus' temptation in the wilderness (Mark 1:12–13, Matt 4: 1–11, Luke 4: 1–13) contains a number of echoes of the story of Israel's wilderness wanderings after the exodus from Egypt. Draw up a chart comparing and contrasting the two stories. See how many points of correspondence you can find.

---

12. Watts, CNTOT, 155–58. I am grateful to my student Richard Rohlfing for bringing the rich scriptural and narrative texture of this parable to my attention.

13. Wright, *Jesus and the Victory of God*, 182.

8

Function

IN THIS FINAL SECTION, we will explore how the Old Testament quotations, allusions and echoes function in the New Testament documents in which they are found. It is often assumed that Old Testament texts were employed by the New Testament writers to support and back up the points they were asserting concerning God's work in Christ. But in recent years the attention given to scriptural intertextuality has challenged this assumption. Many scholars now see that the scriptures of Israel exercise a much more constituative or formative role in the thinking of the writers and the writing of their documents. Thus Paul, Luke, Matthew and John, etc. were not treating the Old Testament so much as a collection of useful authoritative texts but rather as a continuous story, and that their writings are shaped by long study and meditation on the scripture as a whole and on individual texts.

It is not uncommon to find in even the best of modern commentaries on the New Testament a tendency to view citations of the Old Testament as playing a supportive role in the argument of the book rather than a formative or constitutive one. Scripture functions as a support to the argument, rather than as the "subtructure" of New Testament theology. For example J.A Fitzmyer, in his important commentary on Romans, notes that Paul cites scripture to "bolster his view" or "to aid his argument." [1] By contrast, Richard Hays has noted that the scripture plays a much more "constitutive" and creative role in the shaping of the argument in Romans. In a pioneering article Hays has demonstrated that in Rom3:20, where Paul alludes to Psa 143:2, "no living being will be justified before you," not only the language but the logic of Psalm 143 (LXX 142) has shaped the argument of this section of the letter. The scripture is not brought in here simply to support a point or cap off an argument. It is rather that by long meditation on the righteousness of God as presented throughout Psalm 143 ("hear me in your righteousness," 143:1) that Paul has heard the story of the psalm and is rehearsing it afresh in Romans in the light of Christ. For Paul scripture has not so much been plundered as pondered. [2]

Many scholars, myself included, have benefitted from and followed this "contextual" approach of Dodd, Hays and others. Nevertheless, the close observer must admit that there are places where an Old Testament text is cited by a New Testament writer with apparent disregard for its original context. Two often cited cases are "formula quotations" in the early chapters of Matthew: Matt 1:23 (citing Isa 7:14) and Matt 2:15 (Citing Hos 11:1). Here the contexts are respectively the Assyrian crisis and a look back at the Exodus as Hosea confronts Israel's unfaithfulness. These texts appear not to be read by Matthew with careful attention to the original contexts. Nevertheless, it will be noticed that being placed at the beginning of Matthew's gospel they are programmatic for Matthew's whole agenda. The original referents (God's people under siege and the liberation in the Exodus) are not irrelevant to the overall purpose of the Gospel of Matthew.

It is clear that more study is needed on this issue. It is not sufficient to say in a summary way that the New Testament writers "normally respected the context" of an Old Testament text. Nor is it adequate to assert that they regularly cited a text without regard for the context. A much more nuanced approach to the function of

1. Fitzmyer, *Romans*, 109, 705.

2. Hays, *Echoes*, 51–52.

Old Testament references in the New Testament is called for, where each case is treated on its own merits.

MATTHEW 2:15, "OUT OF EGYPT I HAVE CALLED MY SON"

This citation from Hosea 11 has often struck commentators as more atomistic than contextual. For example, R.E. Brown refers to "the general inapplicability of the Hosea context to Jesus."[3] Peter Enns has recently offered a very thoughtful response to this issue of Matthew's regard for the context of the quotation. He draws the contrast between the "son" brought out of Egypt (looking back to the Exodus) and the "son" who sojourned in Egypt for safety and died and rose again to save others.

> The son in Hosea and the Son in Matthew are a study in contrasts. A young *Israel* came out of Egypt, was disobedient, deserved punishment yet was forgiven by God (see Hos 11:8–11). The boy *Christ* came out of Egypt, led a life of perfect obedience, deserved no punishment, but was crucified—the guiltless for the guilty.[4]

To address the issue of respect for the context too narrowly is to miss the real point of the quotation here and elsewhere. The so-called "formula quotations" in Matthew are better served by the term coined for them in German: *Reflexionszitate*. Here are citations on which Matthew (and his fellow Christians) have expended much theological reflection. In this connection, the words of Brevard Childs, in his under-appreciated volume, *The New Testament as Canon*, are to the point.

> The term "reflexion citation" is helpful in emphasizing the role of the citation in evoking an activity of reflection, meditation and interpretation on the part of the reader in striving to grasp the relationship between Old Testament prophecy and New Testament fulfillment. The

3. Brown, *The Birth of the Messiah*, 220 note 23.

4. Enns, *Three Views*, 200.

> New Testament technique of citing a specific passage is badly misunderstood if one concludes that Matthew's interests are narrowly construed or largely apologetic. Rather, the specific text functions as a transparency into the larger prophetic dimension represented by the entire Old Testament.[5]

Childs' notion that the quotations in Matthew function as transparencies may provide a fresh starting point in a much debated, and often stalemated issue.

RELATED QUESTIONS

Related to the question of whether the scriptures of Israel function primarily in a creative or a supportive role are several other questions which are much debated today. First there is the matter of reader and hearer competence. To what extent could the audiences of Paul, Luke, John and the others be expected to hear the echoes or pick up the references to scripture? Since the level of literacy was estimated to be at best 20%, and was probably closer to 10%, of the population in the Greco-Roman world of the first century, would most people who were addressed by the New Testament authors be able to read, let alone understand their arguments from scripture?

A further question is raised concerning the composition of the churches to which the apostles wrote. Were they largely Gentile? Was there a large Jewish element? The latter could be expected to pick up the references to the Old Testament more easily than the former. If Paul, for example, is writing to a largely Gentile audience in Romans, would they be able to follow his dense arguments from scripture, especially in 9–11? If Peter is addressing a largely Gentile constituency in Asia Minor in 1 Peter, can we expect that his readers (or hearers) would have picked up the many scripture allusions in the letter? Would they hear Psalm 34 in 3:10–12? Would they catch the six allusions to Isa 52:13—53:12 , the fourth Servant Song of Isaiah, in 2:21–25? Deciding on this question of how the scripture would function not just for the writer but for the readers is

5. Childs, *The New Testament as Canon*, 70.

crucial for an adequate assessment of the letter as a whole. Behind this question is a further issue referred to as "The Parting of the Ways." Did the Jewish element in the church remain strong for a long time after the first apostolic generation, or did the church in most places in the Roman Empire become largely Gentile, and thus less attuned to scripture allusions and echoes?[6] My own view is that the Jewish element in the early church remained strong well into the second century in most places, and that the Synagogue influence was an important element in the formation of Christian faith and life during that formative period. [7]

One further question that is beyond the scope of this book, but that may be of considerable interest to its readers, is the validity of the early Christian use of the Old Testament as a model for our own methods in Biblical interpretation. Can we replicate their exegesis? Those wishing to pursue this issue will find a stimulating discussion in Stanley N. Gundry, Kenneth Berding and Jonathan Lunde, *Three Views on the New Testament Use of the Old Testament.*[8]

2 CORINTHIANS 4:13

These questions come into sharper focus through a study of 2 Cor 4:13. This verse has received considerable scholarly attention in recent years. Here Paul quotes from Psa 116:10 (LXX 115:1).

> But just as we have the same spirit of faith that is in accordance with the Scripture—"I believed, and so I spoke"—we also believe, and so we speak.

Christopher Stanley has argued that although Paul follows the LXX wording precisely, he "diverges so far from the original context as to raise questions about Paul's reliability as an interpreter."[9] On the other side, Richard Hays proposes a Christological reading of this verse and its context, which is treated by Paul as self-evident.

6. Dunn, *Parting*

7. Stark, *The Rise of Christianity*, 49–71.

8. Grand Rapids: Baker House, 2008.

9. Stanley, "Paul's 'Use,'" 147, see also *Arguing*, 98–101.

He adds, "If it is less so for belated readers twenty centuries later, that is because we lack the necessary hermeneutical key."[10] The "key" for Hays is that Christ is the ultimate speaker of Israel's laments and praises in the Psalms.

So the issue is joined, and several writers have weighed in over the past few years. Both Douglas Campbell and Kenneth Schenck have argued for a Christological reading of the verse and the whole Psalm, suggesting that Paul quoted the text with his own thoughtful reading of the Psalm.[11] On the other hand, Jan Lanbrecht has argued recently that Paul here presents "a simple comparative understanding: Paul has the same state of mind and the same spirit of faith as the psalmist. No attention appears to be given to the psalmist's narrative."[12]

How will you decide on this issue? Was Paul simply lifting a Psalm verse useful for his purposes, or has his citation of it grown out of a meditation on the whole of Psalm 116, and the verse in its context? I suggest that the student look at Paul's use of Psa 116:10 through the various different lenses for studying the Old Testament in the New that we have reviewed in this book. Here are some pointers, based on the chapters of this book, that may aid you in your own investigation.

Form: Note carefully the text form of the quotation. M. Silva lists the text form as agreeing with both the MT and the LXX.[13] But we note that there is some disagreement about the text form, and scholars point out that the Hebrew is uncertain. The NRSV reads for Psa 116:10, "I kept my faith even when I said, 'I am greatly afflicted.'" The REB reads "I was sure I would be swept away; my distress was bitter." Blanket statements about the text form do not give the whole story. Furthermore, the careful student will notice that there is a textual variant within this quotation. An "and" (καὶ) is found in some manuscripts of 2 Corinthians. So Paul's quotation may have read, "I believed, and so I *also* spoke." A few modern

---

10. Hays, *Conversion*, 108–9

11. Campbell, *JBL* (128) 2009, 337–56, Schenck, *CBQ*, 70 (2008) 524–37.

12. Lambrecht, *Method*, 441–48.

13. Silva, *DPL*, 631.

editors have considered this the original reading in 2 Corinthians. (Tischendorf, Kilpatrick). Does this reading have a bearing on Paul's understanding and use of Psalm 116?

Introduction: Paul's introductory formula in 2 Cor 4:13 is unusual: "But just as we have the same spirit of faith that is in accordance with the scripture –." M.Threall wrote in her commentary on 2 Corinthians that Paul, "introduces his quotation with some ceremony. . . which suggests that the psalm verse is of some significance to him."[14] But if Paul is citing the LXX, as is likely, then he is using the first verse of LXX Psalm 115.[15] There is evidence that both before and after the time of Jesus, when Jewish writers cited the first verse (called the *incipit*) the whole Psalm was in view.[16]

Selection: Under this heading we should consider that Psalm 116 was one of the Hallel Psalms (Psalms 113–118), those Psalms sung by Pilgrims to Jerusalem at the Passover. This, then, would have been one of the Psalms sung by Jesus and his disciples at the institution of the Lord's supper. Furthermore, Richard Hays has proposed that this is one of those Psalms in which Christ is seen as the speaker, in accordance with an early Christian convention. This is suggested by the movement from abasement to praise, and by the "prefiguration of the Lord's supper as a means of proclaiming the Lord's death," as seen in verse 13: "I will lift up the cup of salvation and call on the name of the Lord." [17]

Application: In 2 Corinthians 4, Psa 116:10 is employed by Paul as scriptural support for his apostolic ministry. But if the whole Psalm had already been interpreted in the church as a Psalm of the righteous suffering Messiah, then Paul has taken a Christological passage of scripture and applied it to his own ministry. It is interesting to note that Paul makes this move on another occasion. In Rom 15:20–21 Paul takes a central Christological passage (Isaiah 53) and applies it to his own ministry:

---

14. Thrall, *2 Corinthinthians*, I, 304.

15. *NETS*, 605.

16. Carey, *Cry*, 106–11.

17. Hays, *Conversion*, 108–09.

20.Thus I make it my ambition to proclaim the good
news, not where Christ
has already been named, so that I do not build on someone else's foundation,
21. But as it is written:
"Those who have never been told
of him shall see,
and those who have never
heard of him shall
understand." (Isa 52:15).

Combination: While there are no Old Testament citations in
the immediate verses surrounding 2 Cor 4:13, it would be a mistake
to consider the quotation from Psa 116:1 without reference to other
scripture references in the early chapters of the letter. It is interesting to note that in the near context (2 Cor 4:6) Paul alludes to Gen
1:3, "Then God said, 'Let there be light.'" Paul may well be connect-
ing the first speech of God in scripture to his own call to speak the
Gospel. This observation invites further exploration.

History: Although we have no specific quotation from
Psa116:10 in the literature of second temple Judaism, it is interesting to note the reference to the Psalm in connection with the Passover celebration in the Mishna (Pesachim 10:1–9). Here we have a
report on the way the meal was ordered. Four cups were raised and
blessed during the course of the meal. Psalms 115–118 were recited
in connection with the fourth cup. Here Psalm 116 supplied the
reference to the "cup of salvation." James L. Mays wrote about this
pascal use of the Psalm:

> The recitation of the psalms was introduced by a thanks-
> giving to the Lord, who brought us from bondage to free-
> dom, from sorrow to gladness, and from mourning to a
> Festival day, and from darkness to great light, and from
> servitude to redemption (Pesachim 10:5).[18]

The Mishna, of course, post-dates the New Testament. But
the material about the celebration of the Passover must certainly
have a long tradition history, and it is unlikely that Paul would have

18. Mays, *Psalms*, 371.

quoted any verse from Psalm 116, or any of the Hallel psalms without having the story of the Passover and Exodus in mind.

Story: Ask yourself how this quotation in 2 Corinthians fits into the grand narrative of God and his people that Paul is assuming throughout, and telling by his deft use of Old Testament quotations, allusions and echoes.

FOR FURTHER EXPLORATION

Try out for yourself this model of studying a quotation from the Old Testament in the New. Take, for example, another quotation found in 2 Corinthians. It is at 2 Cor 6:1–2:

> 1. As we work together with him, we urge you also not to accept the grace of God in vain, 2 for he says,
> "At an acceptable time I have listened to you,
> and on the day of salvation I have helped you."
> See, now is the acceptable time; see, now is the day of salvation!

Look at this quotation through the eight lenses presented in this book, and see what you uncover:

Form:

Introduction:

Selection:

Application:

Combination:

History:

Story:
Function:

A CONCLUDING INVITATION AND WARNING

The eight chapters of this book have offered a variety of different lenses through which to view the New Testament use of the Old

Testament. It is my hope that by a creative use of these lenses you will deepen your own understanding and appreciation of this captivating subject. At first, this study may seem like a maze, with so much material and so many possible lines of inquiry and ways of interpretation. But with steady practice you will learn to find your way. In the process, you may also find yourself captivated.

I remember once when I was serving a small church in the Peak District of Derbyshire, England, I told one of the local merchants that I was going to take my family to see the maze at Chatsworth House. He looked at me and asked, "Well, you will get in, but will you get out?" The same question may be asked concerning the study of the Old Testament in the New. "You can get in, but will you get out?"

Bibliography

Abegg, M. P. Flint, and E. Ulrich. *The Dead Sea Scrolls Bible: The Oldest Known Bible*. San Francisco: Harper San Francisco, 1999.

Bailey, K. E. *Finding the Lost: Cultural Keys to Luke 15*. St. Louis: Concordia, 1992.

——. *Jacob & the Prodigal: How Jesus Retold Israel's Story*. Downers Grove, Ill.: InterVarsity Press, 2003.

Bauckham, R. "Reading Scripture as a Coherent Story." in *The Art of Reading Scripture*, edited by E. F. Davis and R. B. Hays, 38–53. Grand Rapids: Eerdmans, 2003.

Beale, G. K. and D. A. Carson. *Commentary on the New Testament Use of the Old Testament*. Grand Rapids: Baker Academic, 2007.

Bowker, J.W. "Speeches in Acts: A Study in Proem and Yelammedenu Form." *NTS* 14 (1967) 96–111.

Boyarin, D. *The Jewish Gospels: The Story of the Jewish Christ*. New York: The New Press, 2012.

Brown, R. E. *The Birth of the Messiah: A Commentary on the Infancy Narratives in the Gospels of Matthew and Luke*. New York: Doubleday, 1993.

Bruce, F. F. *This Is That: The New Testament Development of Some Old Testament Themes*. Exeter: Paternoster, 1968.

Campbell, D.A. "2 Corinthians 4:13." *JBL* 128 (2009) 337–56.

Carey, H. J. *Jesus' Cry from the Cross: Towards a First-Century Understanding of the Intertextual Relationship between Psalm 22 and the Narrative of Mark's Gospel*, New York: T & T Clark, 2009.

Childs, B. S. *The New Testament as Canon: An Introduction*. Philadelphia: Fortress Press, 1985.

Davies, P. R. and B. Chilton, "The Akedah: A Revised Tradition History," *CBQ*, 40 (1978) 514–46

Davis, E. F. and R. B. Hays. *The Art of Reading Scripture*. Grand Rapids: Eerdmans, 2003.

DiMattei, S. "Biblical Narratives" in *As It Is Written: Studying Paul's Use of Scripture*, edited by S.E. Porter and C. D. Stanley, 59–93. Atlanta: SBL, 2008.

Dodd, C. H. *According to the Scriptures: The Sub-Structure of New Testament Theology*. London: Nisbet, 1952.

Doeve, J. W. *Jewish Hermeneutics in the Synoptic Gospels and Acts*. Assen: Van Gorcum, 1954.

Dunn, J. D. G. "Jews and Christians: The Parting of the Ways, A.D. 70 to 135:" *The Second Durham-Tübingen Research Symposium on Earliest Christianity and Judaism, Durham, September 1989*. Grand Rapids: Eerdmans. 1999.

Ellis, E. E. *Prophecy and Hermeneutic in Early Christianity: New Testament Essays*. Grand Rapids: Eerdmans, 1978.

———. *The Old Testament in Early Christianity: Canon and Interpretation in the Light of Modern Research*. Tübingen: J.C.B. Mohr, 1991.

Enns, P. *Exodus Retold: Ancient Exegesis of the Departure from Egypt in Wis 10:15–21 and 19:1–9*. Atlanta: Scholars Press, 1997.

Etheridge, J. W. *The Targums of Onkelos and Jonathan Ben Uzziel on the Pentateuch, with the Fragments of the Jerusalem Targum from the Chaldee*. New York: Ktav, 1968.

Evans, C. A. "Jewish Exegesis." In *DTIB*, 380–84.

Evans C. A. and E. Tov. *Exploring the Origins of the Bible*. Grand Rapids: Baker Academic, 2008.

Fishbane, M. *JPS Bible Commentary: Haftarot*. London: Jewish Publication Society, 2002.

———. *Biblical Interpretation in Ancient Israel*, Oxford: Oxford University Press, 1985.

Fitzmyer, J. A. *The Gospel According to Luke: Introduction, Translation, and Notes*. AB 28 New York: Doubleday, 1981.

———. *Romans: A New Translation with Introduction and Commentary*. AB 33, New York: Doubleday, 1993.

García Martìnez, F. *The Dead Sea Scrolls Study Edition*. Leiden: Brill, 1998.

Green, J. B. *The Gospel of Luke*. Grand Rapids: Eerdmans. 1997.

Hay, D. M. *Glory at the Right Hand: Psalm 110 in Early Christianity*. Nashville: Abingdon, 1973.

Hays, R. B. *Echoes of Scripture in the Letters of Paul*. New Haven: Yale University Press, 1989.

———. *The Conversion of the Imagination: Paul as Interpreter of Israel's Scripture*. Grand Rapids: Eerdmans, 2005.

Hooker, M. D. "Did the Use of Isaiah 53 to Interpret His Mission Begin with Jesus?" In Bellinger, W. H. and W. R. Farmer. *Jesus and the Suffering Servant: Isaiah 53 and Christian Origins*. 88–103. Harrisburg, Pa.: Trinity, 1998.

Jobes, K. H. *1 Peter*. Grand Rapids, MI: Baker Academic, 2005.

Jobes, K. H. and M. Silva. *Invitation to the Septuagint*. Grand Rapids: Baker, 2000.

Juel, D. *Messianic Exegesis: Christological Interpretation of the Old Testament in Early Christianity.* Philadelphia: Fortress, 1988.

Käsemann, E. and G. W.Bromiley. Tr. *Commentary on Romans.* Grand Rapids: Eerdmans, 1980.

Kaiser, W. C., K. Berding, D. L. Bock, and P. Enns. *Three Views on the New Testament Use of the Old Testament.* Grand Rapids: Zondervan, 2009.

Keesmaat, S. C. *Paul and His Story: (Re)Interpreting the Exodus Tradition.* Sheffield: Sheffield Academic, 1999.

Lambrecht, J. "A Matter of Method: 2 Cor 4, 13 in the Recent Studies of Schenck and Campbell." *Ephemerides Theologicae Lovaniensis* 86 (2010) 441–48.

Levenson, J. D. *The Death and Resurrection of the Beloved Son: The Transformation of Child Sacrifice in Judaism and Christianity.* New Haven: Yale University Press, 1993.

Lindars, B. *New Testament Apologetic: The Doctrinal Significance of the Old Testament Quotations.* London: SCM, 1961.

Longenecker, R. N. *Biblical Exegesis in the Apostolic Period.* Grand Rapids: Eerdmans, 1974.

Mays, J. L. *Psalms.* Louisville: John Knox Press, 1994.

McNamara, M. *Targum and Testament; Aramaic Paraphrases of the Hebrew Bible: A Light on the New Testament.* Shannon: Irish University Press, 1972.

Metzger, B. M. *A Textual Commentary on the Greek New Testament.* Stuttgart; Deutsche Bibelgesellschaft; United Bible Societies, 1994.

Miller, M., B. S. Halliday, and L. Lushington. *Chartres Cathedral.* New York: Riverside. 1996.

Moyise, S. *Paul and Scripture.* Grand Rapids, Mich.: Baker Academic, 2010.

Pao, D. W. *Acts and the Isaianic New Exodus.* Grand Rapids: Baker Academic, 2002.

Perrin, N. *Jesus the Temple.* Grand Rapids: Baker Academic, 2010.

Pietersma, A. and B.G. Wright, editors. *A New English Translation of the Septuagint and Other Translations Traditionally Included Under That Title.* New York, Oxford: Oxford University Press, 2007.

Porter, S. E. and C. D. Stanley. *As It Is Written: Studying Paul's Use of Scripture.* Atlanta: SBL, 2008.

Rius-Camps, J. and J. Read-Heimerdinger. *The Message of Acts in Codex Bezae: A Comparison with the Alexandrian Tradition.* London: T & T Clark International, 2004.

Rodgers, P. *Text and Story: Narrative Studies in New Testament Textual Criticism.* Eugene: Pickwick Publications, 2011.

Russell, D.A. *Quintilian: The Orator's Education, III, Books 6–8, Loeb Classical Library no. 126.* Cambridge, Ma.: Harvard University Press, 2002.

Sanders, J. A. "From Isaiah 61 to Luke 4." In *Luke and Scripture,* edited by C.A. Evans and J.A. Sanders, 75–106. Eugene, Wipf and Stock, 2001.

Schenck, K. "2 Corinthians and the Pistis Christou Debate." *CBQ* 70 (2008) 524–37.

Bibliography

Stanley, C. D. *Arguing with Scripture: The Rhetoric of Quotations in the Letters of Paul*. New York: T & T Clark International, 2004.

Stark, R. *The Rise of Christianity: How the Obscure, Marginal Jesus Movement Became the Dominant Religious Force in the Western World in a Few Centuries*. San Francisco: HarperSanFrancisco, 1997.

Thrall, M. E. *A Critical and Exegetical Commentary on the Second Epistle to the Corinthians*. Edinburgh: T. & T. Clark, 1994.

Vermes, G. "Bible and Midrash: Early OT Exegesis," in *CHB* I:199–231.

————. *The Complete Dead Sea Scrolls in English*. London: Penguin, 2004.

————. *Jesus in His Jewish Context*. Minneapolis: Fortress Press, 2003.

————. *Scripture and Tradition in Judaism; Haggadic Studies*. Leiden: Brill, 1961.

Watts, R. E. *Isaiah's New Exodus in Mark*. Grand Rapids: Baker, 2000.

Wright, N. T. *The New Testament and the People of God*. Minneapolis: Fortress Press, 1992.

————. *Jesus and the Victory of God*. Minneapolis: Fortress Press, 1996.

————. *The Challenge of Jesus: Rediscovering Who Jesus Was and Is*. Downers Grove: InterVarsity Press, 1999.

————. *Mark for Everyone*. Louisville: SPCK, Westminster John Knox Press, 2004.

————. *Paul: In Fresh Perspective*. Minneapolis: Fortress Press, 2005.